SAXBY'S

1904-2004
CELEBRATING 100 YEARS

A CENTURY IN THE BAKING

SOME LITTLE PIGS—
            GO TO MARKET

BUT THE BEST—
            GO TO SAXBYS

SAXBY'S

1904-2004

CELEBRATING 100 YEARS

A CENTURY IN THE BAKING

ANTHONY SAXBY

SAXBY BROS
WELLINGBOROUGH

We recommend

SAXBY'S

· A SILVER LINK BOOK ·

from

The NOSTALGIA *Collection*

First published in 2004

Frontispiece Saxby's first Gold Medal for pork pies, won in London in 1908 (see page 12).

British Library Cataloguing in Publication Data

A catalogue record for this book is available from the British Library.

ISBN 1 85794 244 2

Silver Link Publishing Ltd
The Trundle
Ringstead Road
Great Addington
Kettering
Northants NN14 4BW

Tel/Fax: 01536 330588
email: sales@nostalgiacollection.com
Website: www.nostalgiacollection.com

Printed and bound in Great Britain

The author extends grateful thanks to Northamptonshire Newspapers, and his colleague and cousin Michael Bell, for their kind permission to reproduce several photographs in this book.

Contents

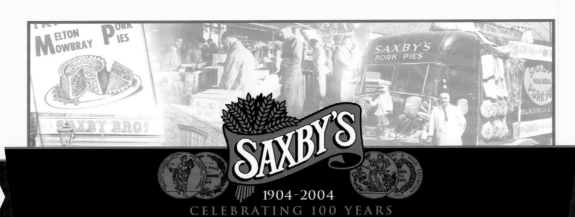

SAXBY'S

1904-2004
CELEBRATING 100 YEARS

A Century In The Baking...

Saxby's is a name synonymous with traditional English savoury baking and the world renowned MELTON MOWBRAY pork pie.

Back in 1904 our founders, Herbert and Ted Saxby, opened their first shop, put 'Pork Butchers' over the door and put Wellingborough, Northamptonshire on the map. Fresh meat was bought in the small hours at London's Smithfield Market and goods delivered by pony and trap to those unable to make the journey to the village store. QUALITY has always been worth paying for and even back then, people were happy to spend a shilling on a delicious SAXBY'S Veal and Ham Pie and children would save their pennies for an individual tupp'ny pork pie. By 1908 the Saxby's insistence on quality was beginning to pay off. We had already been awarded the first of many gold medals and a booming business enabled us to build

Herbert and Ted Saxby came from a family of 11 brothers and sisters born to a tailor from Irchester, John Henry Saxby and his wife Jane

the company's first factory, which opened in 1912 with just 20 workers. By 1921, with a wholesale business and regular deliveries to the discerning stockists and pantries of London, a MODEL FACTORY was opened and the unique taste of Saxby's became appreciated far and wide.

In a CENTURY of trading, we have won over one hundred awards and diplomas for our mouth-watering products, at least one for every memorable year. We have also won a LOYAL following from customers around the UK, for not only our pies but also our chilled pastry, which was launched in 1962.

Things have changed since 1904, but the taste of a Saxby's pie remains instantly and deliciously recognisable. It's a proud tradition that is kept alive by the 4th generation of Saxby's, now taking us into another century of excellence.

In 1921 production was moved to a new model factory in Brook Street East, half a mile from the shop

The packing room in 1932. Saxby's vans went daily to London, 3 times a week to Birmingham and orders from farther afield were sent by rail from Wellingborough station

Saxby's Centenary Certificate 2004

Introduction

It is quite an achievement for any company to continue to trade successfully, in the same family ownership, for one hundred years, and we are one of only a select number of businesses to have done so. We at Saxby's are proud to have reached our centenary, and this book is a celebration of that achievement, recording some of the important, and maybe some of the less important, milestones we have passed along the way.

It is a great privilege and pleasure, as well as something of a responsibility, to be given the opportunity to put together this collection of photographs, memories, advertisements and other archive material reflecting the history of Saxby's over the last one hundred years. Our century has been reached with, inevitably, a degree of good fortune, but also with a huge amount of hard work, dedication and good judgement from all four of the generations of the Saxby family to have so far been involved.

First, of course, were our founders, my grandfather Herbert Saxby senior and his brother, Ted Saxby. They had the skill, commitment and foresight to set up the business all those years ago, to enable it to grow, and to structure it in a way that would allow it to prosper for a century.

The second generation, Herbert junior, Bill and Frank, committed their working lives to developing the business so successfully, especially through the 1950s, '60s and '70s as the retail world began its transformation from local stores to superstores.

More recently, my colleagues of today, the third and fourth generation family members and work colleagues who have worked with me, some for more than 25 years, have grown and evolved the business to meet the challenges of the 1980s, '90s and the new millennium.

We could not have been reached our centenary without the efforts of so many other people, our present and former employees, who have given us a huge part of their lives through the decades. The Saxby story is about these people too, and we thank them for their contribution. I am delighted that some of them feature in this record.

Finally, a 'thank you' to all the people who have helped me to assemble this book by sharing their thoughts and memories of time at Saxby's. They have added so much colour and detail to this record.

This, then, is our story.

Herbert Saxby

Ted Saxby

Above right The founders of the house of Saxby were Herbert and Ted Saxby, two of a family of 11 brothers and sisters born to a tailor from Irchester, John Henry Saxby, and his wife Jane. This remarkable photo, taken in Wellingborough in 1898, shows all 11 dressed in their Sunday best. Back row, left to right, are Dora, Herbert, Rowland and Edward (Ted); middle row, Tom, Bessie, Lottie, Chrissie and Charlie; and in front, George and Mary. Each one has their own fascinating story to tell, but for our purposes we must concentrate on just two, Herbert and Ted.

Right The exact origins of this photograph are unknown: it is entitled 'Saxby Brothers 1899', and is believed to have been taken at a time when four of the Saxby brothers worked together in a butchery business of some sort. Standing, left to right, are unknown, Mr Tucker, G. Russell; Edward (Ted) Saxby, Herbert Saxby senior, and Mr Harper. Seated are G. W. (George) Saxby, unknown, Charles Saxby, and unknown. The boy standing on the wall at the back is thought to be a very young Herbert Saxby junior. The seeds of the new business had been sown.

Herbert, born in 1870, started work when he was 12. Bakers, grocers and coal merchants all employed him, and he also worked for his wife Jane's family at the Parsons pork pie factory in Irchester, where he learned skills that were to be so valuable to him later. He spent some time working in the bakery and butchery trades, serving for a number of years in London. Using his own phrase, one that has filtered down through the Saxby generations, he 'looked after the pennies and let the pounds look after themselves' until he was in his 30s.

One of the original staff in 1904 was a youngster called Sydney Mitchell. He is not in the photo, but his is a fascinating story. The following is an extract from an article about him in *Counter Wise*, the Official Journal of the Grocers' and Provision Dealers' Association, in December 1956:

'During the week of King Edward VII's Coronation young Mitchell moved to Wellingborough (from Kettering) and there commenced quite a long period of service with the famous pie firm of Saxby Brothers, starting with them on the first day that the Wellingborough business was opened. He was paid 1s 6d a week for the job of "gravying" the pies. Leaving school at the age of 14 he commenced his apprenticeship with the firm, in three years his wages rising in 2-shilling increments from 4s to 8s per week. Having completed his apprenticeship he applied for an increase and was awarded a man's wage of 11s per week, coupled with an injunction that now he was receiving a man's wage he would be expected to do a man's work.

His first job was the slaughter of two pigs.

At the age of 17, he transferred to the factory at Luton, where he "lived in" with Mr Edward Saxby. When mentioning this, Mr Mitchell paused and said he would like to pay tribute to the late Mr Herbert Saxby. Mr Saxby was a real taskmaster, added Mr Mitchell, but he provided him with a wonderful training.

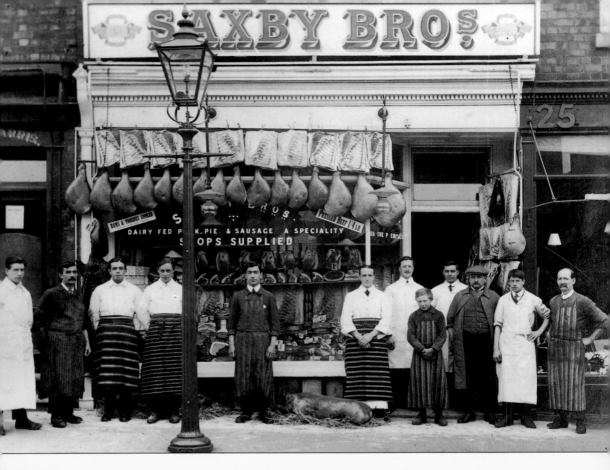

After spending two years at Dunstable, Mr Mitchell then came to work for the firm in London. This was in 1912, and the 1914/18 war caught up with him and he served as a Petty Officer Steward. There were many famous naval actions during World War 1 and ex-PO Mitchell is proud to have been a participant in at least one of them.

On demobilisation, Mitchell returned to Civvy Street and to Saxby's at Golders Green, where he remained for over 13 years. In 1932 he left and opened S. W. Mitchell's butcher's shop at The Hyde, Hendon.'

Mr Mitchell's apprenticeship must have been well served, because he went on to build a successful business of his own.

At the age of 34, with cash in the bank and a desire to be his own boss, Herbert teamed up with his younger brother Ted, who was by then living in Luton. They bought their first shop, at 23 Midland Road, Wellingborough, in 1904. They put 'Pork Butchers' over the door, and quickly gained a reputation for the quality of their products. They made the pies in a room upstairs and sold them downstairs. 'It was hard work, but we got a living from the start,' Herbert recalled in a later interview celebrating his 84th birthday.

This photograph was taken in 1912. Among those in the group are Herbert Saxby junior again (fourth from the left), and Mr Bill Lawrence (third from the left), who later became Foreman and who appears several times later in this book. The gentleman on his own in the centre is Len Chapman, who went on to celebrate his own centenary, his 100th birthday, in 1991. Also in the picture are George Saxby senior, William Coles, Les Foster, F. Templeman, and old George, who was the pigman from Little Irchester.

Note the dry-cured hams, branded 'SAXBYS', and the flitches of bacon, together with the gaslight in the foreground and the pig in straw on the pavement.

Above From the outset, the brothers set out to be the very best of pork pie makers. They soon began entering national competitions, and this Bronze Medal Certificate is the earliest record we have of their success. The event was the Universal Cookery & Food Exhibition, and was 'Under the Special Patronage of Her Majesty The Queen'. This presumably was Queen Alexandra. Held at the Royal Horticultural Hall, Westminster, on 2-5 May 1905, the Bronze Medal was awarded to 'Messrs Saxby Bros for the General Excellence of their Exhibit in Class 37 – Pork Pies etc'.

Below left Our first Gold Medal for pork pies was won at the Confectioners' Bakers' and Allied Traders' Annual International Exhibition in the Royal Agricultural Hall, London, on 12 September 1908. The citation reads: 'This is to Certify that Saxby Bros, Wellingborough, is awarded a Gold Medal (1st Prize) for Pork Pies, Class 41.' Competitions have played an important part in the company's development over the years, and we have since won well over 100 Gold Medals and Diplomas for our products, more of which later.

Below This early advert for Saxby's Pies appeared in the *Wellingborough News* in 1910, and the 1908 Gold Medal for excellence is of course featured. Sausages were 9d per pound (about 4p today) and veal and ham pies from 1 shilling (5p). The shop opened for long hours, often staying open until 9.00pm on Fridays and midnight on Saturdays. Note the phone number: 19x5.

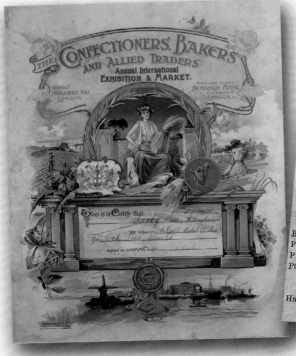

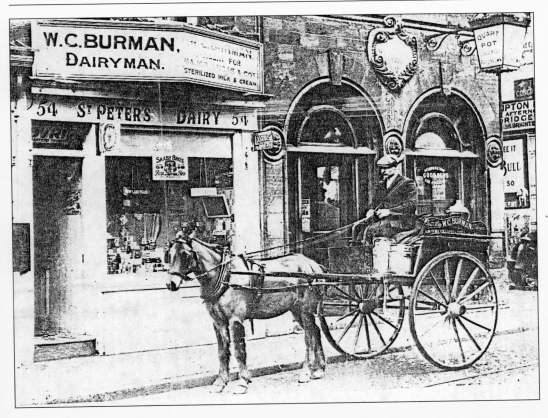

Right Even in those early days, Saxby's pies were sold to other retailers. This photograph, taken in about 1910, shows Burman's Dairy at 54 Marefair, Northampton, with a poster in the window advertising 'Saxby Bros Pork Pies'.

The hard work was paying off, and in 1912 the brothers bought a small factory behind their shop, at Glenbank. Records show that 20 people worked there. Most of the meat came from London's Smithfield Market: Herbert used to catch the first train to London, the 3.17am, make his deals on the market at dawn, and be back in Wellingborough in time to open the shop at 9.00am.

Below Herbert bought his new home, The Lindens, in Midland Road, at around this time. This substantial house became the centre for many family and business occasions over the next 50 years.

· 2 ·
The 1920s and 1930s
A new factory

Below There is no record of events at Saxby's during the days of the First World War. It was a period of containment for the brothers. However, we do know that Herbert junior served in the Army during the war, and this photo is of his welcome home party, given on the lawns of The Lindens. The formal invitation read:

Messrs H. & E. Saxby
Request the pleasure of your company
To a Dinner and Social Evening
To commemorate the homecoming of
Herbert Saxby, jun., and other members of the firm,
to be held on 26th December 1918 at 5.30pm.

Herbert is standing, fifth from the right, pipe in hand. The boy in short trousers, bottom right, is his brother Frank.

Right After the war the firm could at last start to think about the future again. On their travels the brothers had got to know many people, and made many contacts within the trade both locally and further afield. This convinced them that there was a demand for their products outside Wellingborough, and they decided that the time was right to expand. The partnership was restructured and a limited company, Saxby Bros Limited, was formed. Here are the original Certificate of Incorporation dated the Seventh day of December 1920, and Herbert junior's share certificate, dated 29 December, granting him 100 £1 shares, signed by both the founders.

Below From now on, the wholesale business in London and up and down the British Isles began to build up. This development, and winning more prizes at other national trade competitions, further enhanced Saxby's growing reputation. This created an even greater demand, and it was clear to the brothers that they needed to move to larger premises. They purchased a 4-acre plot of land opposite The Lindens, in Brook St. East, some half a mile from the shop. Construction began in 1920, and in 1921 production was moved to the new 'model' factory. This is the oldest picture we have showing the exterior of the new factory, although it was actually taken a few years later, in 1934 – more is said about the fleet of vehicles on page 21. The succeeding generations are grateful to our founders that they had the foresight to purchase such a large plot. At the time they only used less than a quarter of the total area; it has taken us another 80 years to fill up the remainder.

The handwritten ledger reads:

Balance Sheet — 2nd February, 1922.

Liabilities

			Assets		
Share Capital	8480		To Goodwill of Business		780
Directors' Fees	1348 12 10		Stocks on Hand		3193
Sundry Creditors	3293 16 6		Accounts on Hand		2784 11 7
Amount due to Bank	4663 18 8		Cash on Hand		422 16 10
Balance - Profit & Loss account	2295 15 8		Fixture Account :-		
			Value 2nd February, 1921	4167 17 7	
			additions	641 12 3	
				4809	
			Depreciation	380 5	4428 15
			New Factory :-		
			Costs to 2nd February 1921	7065 2 7	
			additions	541 13 5	
				7606 16	
			Depreciation	3 16	7603
	£ 19157 3 5				£ 19157 3 5

Above This significant investment marked the beginning of a new era for the business. New accounting standards were introduced, and we still have the ledgers of account from 1922 onwards. This extract from the Balance Sheet and Trading Account for the year to 2 February 1922 shows that the cost of the new factory was £7,606 16s 0d. Sales for the year were £90,790, and the gross profit was £14,932. Among the costs for that year was 'Horse Keep £145/3/8'.

Below left This fascinating photo, taken in 1922, shows the full operation of the new bakery. This is the same space where many Saxby's pies are made today, though there the comparison ends!

In the background can be seen the meat being prepared and minced. The pastry is being mixed by machines driven by huge belts, and there are also machines for dividing the dough into small pieces. On the tables the full process of hand-making a Melton Mowbray Pie can be seen: raising the pie on the wooden block, filling it with meat, sealing the lid and crimping it, and finally placing it into the coke-fired draw-plate oven on the left for baking (see page 47).

On the right is a peel oven, which was also used for pies. The table in the foreground is where the ladies filled the pies with freshly made gelatine stock after baking.

The gentleman in the dark smock with hand on hip – the only person not working – is Herbert Saxby junior, while Ted Saxby is the gentleman wearing braces on the left. Also in the picture are Tom Sewell junior (trimming the pies, right middle), Charlie Thompson (bottom right), Les Foster (oven man, top left), Bill Lawrence, and Charlie Ward. The oven man had to do two jobs: shovelling coke and attending to the burners, as well as operating the ovens.

Above With a new factory to fill, the Directors needed to increase sales by expanding the company's customer list, so they looked to appoint Agents in more distant areas. This extract from a Memorandum of Agreement dated 6 December 1922 appoints Samuel J. Palmer as the company's Traveller and Commission Agent in the Counties of Northumberland, Durham and York.

It is signed on the rear by Herbert Saxby senior (*inset*).

Left As the wholesale business grew, so did the need to advertise. This leaflet, from 1922/23, uses the bakery photo and is the earliest reference we have to Saxby's 'Melton Mowbray' pork pies and veal, ham and egg pies. This distinctive style of pie has become Saxby's hallmark, more of which later. By now, the company had received '20 Awards for Quality', already one of the key values of the business, which has continued through the generations. The phone number is now 168.

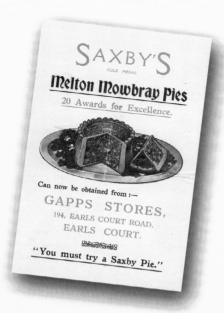

Above It was in 1922 that the company first started wrapping its pies in what one would call proper retail packaging. This advert told customers that 'Saxby's 1-lb Pies are now packed in these Hygienic Boxes assuring cleanliness, eliminating breakages and making them more convenient to carry', surely a definition of the reasons for good packaging today.

Above right By the mid 1920s, when this leaflet was produced, regular daily deliveries were being made to London. The depot, office and shop in Golders Green where Mr Mitchell worked (see page 10) was thriving, and deliveries had commenced to Harrods and Fortnum & Mason. The company targeted the best provision

merchants in each town, and Gapps Stores in Earls Court was the latest new account in 1923.

Below This wonderful display of pies was photographed in the bakery, in front of the draw-plate ovens, in 1926. These were capable of baking 16 large trays of pies at a time. The pies in the picture are all dummies, which were very popular for display purposes. Filled with sawdust and varying in size from 1lb right up to 4lb, 6lb, 8lb, and the largest at 10lb to 12lb, they looked real and lasted for months. The largest ones were formed around circular boxes that had been used to supply cheese rounds, and were made for special events, such as Christmas.

This grainy picture shows, from left to right, Bill Lawrence, Tom Sewell and Charlie Thompson taking a break outside the bottom bakery in 1928. Bill was, you will recall, in the original 1912 shop photo. He was with Saxby's from the start in 1904 and went on to become Foreman, a position he held for 20 years. When he retired in 1958 Tom Sewell took over as Foreman until his retirement in 1967. Both were key members of the management team, much respected by their staff and much relied upon by the Directors. Charlie Thompson was the man in charge of the important job of mixing the dough.

This is the earliest letter on a company letterhead in the archives. It is a reference for Nicholas Hegarty, dated 24 August 1928, and is signed by Miss Chrissie Saxby, one of the two founders' sisters, who worked full time for the business and was in effect the company administrator for many years.

These were hard times, and the staff were expected to work long hours to meet the demand. The company fell foul of the Factory Inspector at Christmas 1926, the following report appearing in the *Daily Chronicle* of 14 February 1927:

'EMPLOYMENT OF GIRLS IN PORK PIE FACTORY. Saxby Bros, pork pie manufacturers, were summoned before the court for employing Violet Bellham, Lily Ingram, and Winifred Abbott in their factory contrary to the provisions of the Factories and Workshops Act at Wellingborough on December 19th, 20th, 21st and 22nd 1926. The evidence would show that the girls worked from 8am on Sunday until between 9.30pm and 1.45am on the following Monday morning. Mr Parker, defending, said that there was a great rush of orders at that time of year and it was practically impossible to run the factory without overtime. Employees were provided with lunch at 11.00am, they had dinner between 12.30 and 1.30, tea at 4.30pm and supper at 8.00pm. They could finish when they liked, and were taken home by motor car in the morning. Mr Saxby said he was sorry, but the workpeople were properly paid and worked of their own free will.

The Bench, after retiring, imposed a fine of £1 in each case, and costs of 14 shillings.'

This wonderful float, at St Albans Carnival in 1923, only managed Third Prize, but it was a pretty impressive effort. By now, Saxby shops had opened in Bedford, Luton and Golders Green, as well as St Albans.

Left The carnival float for 1928 was not quite so lavish. The drivers are David Lawrence and Harry Jarvis.

Below The family enjoyed putting on a good show, and this lovely old vehicle was dressed up for the Wellingborough Carnival in 1926. Note the huge dummy pies on the roof, and the pig carcases on the fenders! The drivers are George Saxby and Harry Jarvis. The photo was taken in Saxby's yard, and the houses in the background, in Chester Rd, are still there.

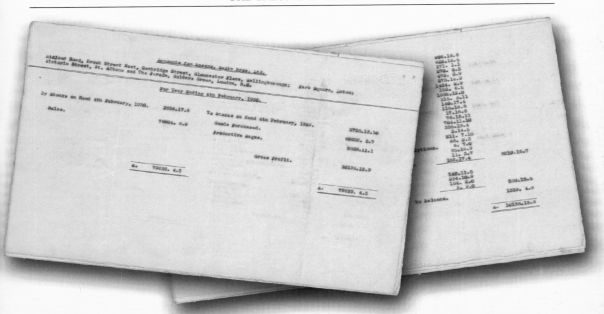

Above The company's official accounts for the year ending 4 February 1930 (audited by accountants Gillitt & Gillitt of Market Square, Wellingborough) indicate sales of £79,639 4s 3d. Gross profit was £10,138 13s 9d, and after deducting all the overhead costs the net profit was £1,339 4s 9d. The address line confirms that there are now six shops – three in Wellingborough (Gloucester Place had opened in 1929, joining Midland Road and Cambridge Street), and Luton, St Albans, and Golders Green. Brook Street East was the wholesale business.

Below This is a close-up of the vehicles in the 1934 photo of the 'new' factory in Brook St East on page 15. By now our distribution network was covering an area far and wide, as these handsome Ford vehicles testify. The London office, in Golders Green, is open for business – note 'Wellingborough' and 'London' on the side panels. Deliveries to London were made daily and pick-ups of meat (from Smithfield Market), bacon, cheese and other provisions for the shops would have made up the return load. Many orders were packed in wicker baskets, such as those on the roof-rack of each vehicle. Sadly, none of these lovely old vehicles remain.

Below Most of the pork used by the company was sourced locally. In the very early days the company had operated a very small pig slaughterhouse in Little Irchester, while another, built on the new site in 1923 and used for bullocks, had been a very primitive affair. By 1931 this proper abattoir was operating. It just handled pigs, and these were purchased at local markets and direct from local farmers. The throughput was about 60 a day, and the methods were still primitive by modern standards. Facing the camera is Bill Mace, while the man wearing a striped apron is Tom Sewell senior.

Bottom This is the bacon curing room in 1931. The pork was very different from that used today – much fatter and heavier.

Right In the same room we see the sausage-making department in action. The tall young man is Frank Saxby, who had joined the business in 1930 after qualifying in farm management at Moulton Agricultural College. On the trolley, back right, is a rack of cooked hams and black puddings, and other small goods.

Below right This was the department that made the 'tupp'ny pies', in the bottom bakehouse, seen in 1929. These were the small 4oz pork pies, which sold for two old pennies each, and the name stuck for the next 60 years. There is not much sign of mechanisation yet, but the pastry was divided on a machine and formed into its pie case by a press. The meat, in the 'bath', was deposited by hand, then a crimping machine sealed on the lid. Among those in the picture are Jock Hardie, on the left, Fred Ashpole and Bert Cartwright. The small lady at the back is 'Mealy' Thompson from Irchester: her job was to put the egg glaze on the finished pies.

Opposite above The ham tinning department, or, as it was called in advertising at the time, the 'New Model Canning Factory', is seen in 1931. Gammons on the trolley to the left are being boned before being placed in tins and sealed in the machine on the right, prior to cooking. Ox tongues and briskets of beef were also canned. This room was always known as the Ham Room and was used for cooking hams right up to the 1980s.

Opposite below This is the packing room in 1932. Saxby's own vehicles delivered to London every day, Birmingham three times a week, and around the local towns and villages as required. More distant destinations were reached by rail, and daily trips to the two Wellingborough stations were needed. Solid wooden boxes were often utilised, having originally been used to import walnuts and dried fruit.

The gentleman in the centre is Frank Saxby again. He, his brother Herbert junior, and their cousin Bill Saxby senior, were now all working full-time in the business.

By 1932 Saxby's pork pies had become nationally recognised, and the company had stockists in most major towns and cities; many London stores were also customers. The major national exhibition was the Ideal Home Exhibition, held annually at Olympia in London. Saxby's decided this year to exhibit for the first time, and these two pictures show the first display stand. The company went on to exhibit at every show for the next 60 years, and further pictures appear later.

Cyril Ashpole first started working for the firm in 1919 and went on to complete 55 years of service. Years later, he reminisced about his experiences during this period: 'I joined the firm in 1919 a year before I left school. I remember standing on a box in Midland Road shop window, cleaning the rails with emery paper. Later, I worked at the factory. All the pork pies went by rail. I took them to the station in a pony and cart. I also did the country round with a pony and cart, to Rushden, Raunds, Yelden and Chelveston.

Cyril also remembered 'going to London on the London van and delivering to Harrods, Barkers, Selfridges and Fortnum & Mason. That was the year 1921.'

Later, he was promoted: 'When Mr Coles retired in 1935, I was put in charge of the despatch department on 35 shillings a week.'

Cyril was a mathematical genius, especially mental arithmetic, and could add up columns of pounds, shillings and pence at a glance. As he remembers, 'I was doing figures all day long, plus invoices. I never used a ready-reckoner. I used to take books home to check, for which I was paid an extra £1 per week.'

Left A new Saxby's shop opened in Abington St, Northampton, on 9 December 1933. The offers weren't bad – spend 5 shillings and get a free 1lb pork pie worth 1s 2d.

Opposite This is the 1933 Christmas brochure for the Northampton shop – each of the other shops would have had its own front page. The colourful illustration on the front was used many times subsequently over the next 30 years. The introduction promises: 'It is our endeavour in this Price List to bring your attention to the outstanding quality and reasonable prices of our Seasonable Specialities. Created to please the palate, Saxby's products will ensure that your Christmas Festivities will be a real success.' There is also a Mail Order Department, offering parcel post delivery of a 5lb parcel for 9d.

Xmas SAXBY'S LIST

Specialists in

Turkeys
Geese
Ducks
Chickens
Xmas Puddings,
Pork Pies, Dairy Fed Pork
Etc., Etc.

SAXBY BROS. LTD.
11, Abington St. Northampton
PHONE 2085   VAN DELIVERIES TO ALL PARTS

PLEASE ORDER EARLY

★MAIL ORDER DEPARTMENT

All Orders are packed and delivered Free of Charge, Mail and Telephone Orders receive careful and prompt attention from a competent staff.

POSTAL INFORMATION
Parcel Post Rates

2 pounds	- -	6d.
5 pounds	- -	9d.
8 pounds	- -	1/-
11 pounds (limit)	-	1/3

WE HAVE DEVOTED
YEARS TO STUDYING
HOW BEST WE CAN
SERVE YOU

Awarded over Twenty Gold Medals and Diplomas for Excellence

IT is our endeavour in this Price List to bring your attention to the outstanding quality and reasonable prices of our Seasonable Specialities.

Created to please the palate, Saxby's products will ensure that your Christmas Festivities will be a real success.

As it is only possible to include a few of our goods, we would welcome a personal visit during which you may inspect our range of foods and select your Christmas Fare.

The Directors would also like to take this opportunity of thanking their many Customers for their kind support during the current year, and ask them to accept our Season's Compliments.

Saxby Bros., Ltd.
11 ABINGTON STREET, NORTHAMPTON
Phone 2085

SAXBY'S POULTRY DEPARTMENT

Prime Young Turkeys

THE PICK OF THE MARKET, DRESSED READY FOR THE OVEN

ENGLISH, 14 to 20 lbs. - from per lb. 1/6
ENGLISH, 8 to 12 lbs. - " " " 1/4
IMPORTED, 12 to 18 lbs. - " " " 1/2
IMPORTED, 6 to 10 lbs. - " " " 11d.
Specially prepared Turkey Stuffing, per lb. 1/-

Special Offer

PRIME YOUNG GEESE. Guaranteed young birds from our Own Farms. 10 to 16 lbs. per lb. 10d.
ENGLISH DUCKS - - - per lb. 1/-

GUARANTEED YOUNG BIRDS
FINEST SELECTION

SAXBY'S POULTRY DEPARTMENT

Prime Young Chickens

OUR OWN KILLING, DRESSED READY FOR THE OVEN

LARGE BIRDS, (6—8 lbs.) - - per lb. 1/3
MEDIUM BIRDS, (3—6 lbs.) - ,, ,, 1/4
IMPORTED (2¼—4 lbs.) - - ,, ,, 1/1

Finest Roast Chickens

Ready for Table, each 2/9

Special Offer

BOILING FOWLS. LARGE BIRDS per lb. 9d.
Sausage Meat Stuffing - - per lb. 1/-

SOMETHING TO
CROW ABOUT
AND WE ARE
GOING TO
SAXBYS.

SAXBY'S BUTCHERY DEPARTMENT

Dairy Fed Pork

PRIME YOUNG PORK FROM LOCAL CHRISTMAS SHOWS

Leg - - - - - - per lb. 1/2
Loin - - - - per lb. 1/- and 1/2
Cuttings - - - - - per lb. 1/-
Streaky - - - - - ,, ,, 9d.
Blade - - - - - ,, ,, 10d.
Hand - - - - - ,, ,, 8d.

Special Offer

SCOTCH LEG MUTTON - per lb. 1/-
,, SHOULDERS ,, - per lb. 10d.

Specially Prepared Sage and Onion Stuffing
6d. and 3d. Packet

THE CHOICEST CUTS
AT REASONABLE PRICES
AT SAXBYS

SAXBY'S PROVISION DEPARTMENT

Prime Hams

FINEST YORK, 12 to 16 lbs. - per lb. 1/6
,, ,, 16 to 20 lbs. - ,, 1/5
PICNIC (4 to 8 lbs.) - - ,, 9d.
SHORT HAMS (from 9 lbs.) per lb. 1/- and 1/1

Selected Danish Bacon

Corner Gammon Joints - from per lb. 1/4
Middle Gammon - - - ,, 1/7
Fore Hock - - from ,, 7d.
PEAT SMOKED IN OUR OWN STOVES

Cheese

Finest Empire Red - per lb. 7d.
Finest English Cheddar - per lb. 1/-
Finest Gorgonzola - - ,, 1/-
SELECTED AND EXCELLENT FLAVOURS

Special Offer

HOME-CURED BACON, (Piece) per lb. 11d.
,, ,, (Sliced) - ,, 1/1
FULLY MATURED. OUR OWN FEEDING AND CURING

SOME LITTLE PIGS—
GO TO MARKET
BUT THE REST—
GO TO SAXBYS

SAXBY'S XMAS SPECIALITIES

Christmas Puddings, Mincemeat

MADE FROM THE ORIGINAL RECIPE WITH EMPIRE
FRUIT, ENGLISH SUET, AND NEW LAID EGGS

1-lb. size - - - - each 1/4
2-lb. size - - - - each 2/6
Large Puddings - - - per lb. 1/2

Mincemeat

OUR OWN MAKE FROM CHOICEST INGREDIENTS
In ½-lb. and 1-lb. Cartons - - per lb. 8d.

Puff Pastry

Delicious and Economical - per lb. 6d.

Special Offer

MINCE PIES, boxes of 6, - - 6d.

THE PROOF
IS IN THE EATING

SAXBY'S COOKED MEATS ETC.

Gold Medal Pork Pies

Large Pies — each 1/2, 1/9, 2/4, 3/6 etc.
Small Pies — each 3d., 6d., and 9d.

ANY SIZE MADE TO ORDER AT 1/2 PER LB.

Sliced Cooked Meats

Ham	per lb. 2/4 and 2/-
Tongue	" " 3/- and 2/4
Brisket of Beef	per lb. 1/8
Roast Pork	" " 2/-
Jellied Veal	" " 1/6
PORK SAUSAGES	per lb. 1/2 and 1/-
BEEF SAUSAGES	per lb. 6d.

Special Offer

COOKED HAM (whole or half) — per lb. 1/10

ONE OF SAXBY'S SKILLED CHEFS

GIVE YOUR FRIEND

A ...

SAXBY HAMPER
THIS CHRISTMAS

These Gifts make a welcome addition to the Christmas Menu and at these special prices make a very acceptable and inexpensive Present.

THE £1 HAMPER CONTAINS:—
1 Turkey (approx. 12 lbs.) 1 lb. Stuffing
One 2-lb. Xmas Pudding. One 2-lb. Pork Pie
One Tin of Fruit.

THE 10/- HAMPER CONTAINS:—
One Large English Chicken (Dressed and Stuffed)
(approx. 4 lbs.)
One 2-lb. Xmas Pudding. One 1-lb. Pork Pie
½-lb. Sausage Meat. One Tin of Fruit

THE 5/- HAMPER CONTAINS:—
One 1-lb. Xmas Pudding. One 2-lb. Pork Pie
1-lb. Best Pork Sausage. One Tin of Fruit

Carefully packed and despatched by us to any address for the cost of postage only.

SAXBY'S FOR QUALITY

11 Abington St, NORTHAMPTON
Phone 2085

FATHER CHRISTMAS PREFERS SAXBY'S

WAYSIDE WISDOM

"There is money in eggs," runs the advertisement slogan—we've never found any.

According to the geologist we are all beggars—we live on the crust of the earth !

Mistress—"Why did you get dismissed from your last place ?"

Jane—"I was so good looking that when I answered the door, people mistook me for the mistress—there's no danger of that here, of course."

Teacher—"What is an herbaceous border ?"

Johnny—"Please miss—a lodger what does'nt eat meat."

To Ice a Christmas Cake—soak it in water and stand outside to freeze.

The 1933 brochure promotes all the usual products. Pork pies are 1s 2d per pound, and Christmas puddings are also being advertised – 'made from the original recipe with Empire fruit, English suet, and new laid eggs' – as well as mincemeat and mince pies. Puff pastry is also on sale, at 6d for a 1lb packet; this is the first time we see it being available to purchase, cooks of any standing previously having been expected to make their own. Short pastry did not become available for many more years, as we shall see later. The illustrations are all great fun, but some would not be regarded as 'politically correct' today!

THE CONTINUED GROWTH OF THE BUSINESS OF SAXBY'S is maintained by the fact that all their products are made with the finest ingredients possible, blended in a way that only their long experience could produce.

¶ For instance, all the Pork for their Pies and Sausages is guaranteed home fed, and killed in their new modern abattoir, by the latest electric Humane Killer, as also is the Veal for their Veal, Ham and Egg Pies.

¶ Therefore, in comparing these prices with those of other houses, consideration should be given to the excellent quality of SAXBY'S PRODUCTS, as departure from this policy would undermine the otherwise permanent goodwill established among their many hundreds of customers during the last thirty years.

SAXBY BROS. LTD.
WELLINGBOROUGH

On the cover page of the 1934 wholesale price list (*left*) the consumer marketing concepts of today were already being promoted with such phrases as 'made with the finest ingredients possible' and 'the pork is guaranteed home fed'. Perhaps less likely to be used by today's marketeers is 'killed in their new modern abattoir, by the latest electronic Humane Killer…'

The eight-page list includes those reproduced here, advertising pies, of course, as well as sausages, hams and other cooked meats, and products such as polony, black pudding, haslet and faggots. On the Melton Mowbray pork pie page (*right*), 1lb and 2lb

AWARDED 20 GOLD MEDALS & DIPLOMAS FOR EXCELLENCE

Saxby's Sausages.

Royal Cambridge Pork -	13/- doz. lb.
Pork - - - -	11/- ,,
Oxford Beef - -	6/6 ,,
Chipolata, 20 links to the lb. -	15/- ,,
Smoked, (6 to the lb.) in display cartons	1/3 per lb.
Beef Luncheon (4—8-lb. bungs) -	7d. ,,
Pork Breakfast (1—3-lb. each) -	1/3 ,,
Liver Sausage (2—4-lb. each) -	1/3 ,,
Polonies	
Polony (Special Yorkshire) -	10d. per lb.
Saveloys - - -	1/- per doz.
Black Puddings -	5d. per lb.
Chicken, Ham and Tongue (about 7-oz.)	6/6 per doz.
Chicken, Ham and Tongue (about 13-oz.)	10/6 ,,

HAMS, BACON, LARD AND DRIPPING

Hams, Home-cured, 16—22-lbs. - -	per cwt.
Bacon, Draft Flitches - -	,,
Lard, Home-rendered -	,,
Lard, Home-rendered in ½lb. and 1lb. cartons,	per doz. lbs.
Pork Dripping in ½-lb. cartons -	5/6 per doz.
Beef Dripping in buckets -	per cwt.
Beef Dripping in ½-lb. and 1-lb. cartons	

AWARDED 20 GOLD MEDALS & DIPLOMAS FOR EXCELLENCE

Saxby's Pies.

MELTON MOWBRAY
VEAL, HAM AND EGG.

1-lb., 1½-lb. and 2-lb.	
oblong shape in display cartons	1/- per lb.
¾-lb. oblong shape in display cartons	9/- per doz.
10 oz. oblong shape in display cartons	7/- per doz.
Pytchley Pies, oval shape, about 10 oz.	6/6 per doz.

PASTRIES.

Steak and Kidney, 5½—6 oz. -	2/- per doz.
Sausage Rolls, large	
in 2 dozen display cartons	1/6 per doz.
Puff Pastry in packets -	5/3 per dozen lbs.
Puff Pastry in packets -	2/9 per dozen ½-lbs.

hand-raised pies are priced at 1 shilling per pound. Individual ¼lb pork pies are 2 shillings a dozen – just 2d each. These were of course the 'tupp'ny pies' again, which would have retailed at 2½d.

Finally, the Terms and Conditions page (*bottom right*) states that 'Orders over 10/- carriage paid by Passenger Train. Goods sent in free boxes or returnable hampers.' Customers were advised that 'consignments should be checked against invoice accompanying goods, and any shortage notified on the Carman's sheet.' They were also requested to 'kindly post orders early enough to allow to be made after receipt of order'.

AWARDED 20 GOLD MEDALS & DIPLOMAS FOR EXCELLENCE

Saxby's Pies.

MELTON MOWBRAY PORK

1-lb., 1½-lb. and 2-lb. Hand Raised -	1/- per lb.
3-lb. and upwards, Hand Raised -	1/1 ,,
¾-lb. Hand Raised -	9/- per doz.
½-lb. Hand Raised -	5/3 ,,
⅓-lb. Machine Made -	4/6 ,,
¼-lb. Hand Raised -	2/6 ,,
¼-lb. Machine Made -	2/3 ,,

All the above made in Veal, Ham and Egg
if required.

GALA PIES

Veal, Ham and Egg, 4-lb., 6-lb. and 7-lb.
1/- per lb.

Made of English Veal suitable for cutting out.

AWARDED 20 GOLD MEDALS & DIPLOMAS FOR EXCELLENCE

Saxby's Cooked Meats.

York Hams (14—22-lbs.)	-	per lb.
Home-cured, trimmed of excessive fat.		
Boneless English Gammons -	-	,,
Boneless Danish Gammons -	-	,,
Boneless Hams -	-	,,
Cooked Gammons (Bone in)	-	,,
Roast English Legs of Pork	2/2	,,
Brisket of Beef (in slabs of 8—14-lbs)	-	,,
Pressed Veal and Ham,		
▢ Shape, (about 9-lbs.) -	1/2	,,
Pressed Pork and Veal,	-	1/3 ,,
(in slabs of 8—14 lbs.)	-	1/4 ,,
Pressed Pork -	-	7d. ,,
Pork Brawn (in moulds of 4—7-lbs.) -	1/2	,,
Veal Brawn (in moulds of 4—7-lbs.)		,,

TINNED GOODS

Ox Tongues, 12 Tins to case,		
6-lb. Tins	-	per case
Tinned Gammons, 6 Tins to case,		
gross for nett. -	-	per lb.
Tinned Brisket of Beef,		
6 Tins to case, gross for nett. -	-	

These are prepared in our New Model Canning Factory by
the latest equipment.

Terms and Conditions of Sale

PAYMENT OF ACCOUNT.
Net Cash on receipt of statement to Head Office, Wellingborough

CARRIAGE.
Orders over 10/- carriage paid by Passenger Train.

PACKAGES.
Goods sent in free boxes or returnable hampers.

CLAIMS.—PILFERAGE AND DAMAGED GOODS.
Unless notified within 3 days of receipt of goods, claims for shortage or damages cannot be entertained.

All consignments should be checked against invoice accompanying goods, and any shortage notified on the Carman's sheet. If impossible to do this, sign Railway sheet "unexamined" and notify the Stationmaster as well as ourselves of the shortage. Failure to do this deprives us of any chance of claims on the Railway Company.

NEW ACCOUNTS.
To prevent any delay, new customers will oblige by sending cash with first orders, or two Wholesale References.

ORDERS AND FRESHNESS OF GOODS.
As there is often delay in post, we advise standing orders. If impossible, kindly post early enough to allow goods to be made after receipt of order.

GUARANTEE.
All goods quoted in this List are hereby guaranteed to be of the nature, substance and quality described, and to conform in every respect with the requirements of the Food and Drugs Act, and all regulations relating to Foodstuffs now in force.

SAXBY BROS. LTD. WELLINGBOROUGH

Above The pre-war Saxby's Ideal Home Exhibition stands were all classics. Space prohibits showing them all, but this 1934 effort and the 1938 display on page 35 are typical. Note the Special Exhibition Size Pie selling at 2 shillings. Saxby's continued to use this special size promotion for more than 50 years.

Below It was not all work for the Saxby family, and in 1934 they managed to field a full cricket XI for a match played against a team of local farmers. The line-up of players, from back left in the photo, was Herbert Saxby junior (Director), Tom Saxby, Frank Saxby (Director), Jack Saxby, Bill Saxby senior (Director), Tom Saxby (brother of the founders), Herbert Saxby senior (founder) Ted Saxby (founder), Rowland Saxby (brother of the founders), Paul Saxby, and George Saxby junior. The umpires were Stan Collier and E. Jones.

Above In 1936 this Saxby retailer – The Delicatessen of Apsley, Hemel Hempstead – entered the Daily Express National Window Display Competition. The 'Help Your Neighbour' campaign slogan was 'Every penny spent here helps to reduce Unemployment', but it is unclear precisely how this was achieved. The Saxby slogan on the shield on the right might possibly be challenged by today's nutritionalists – 'Good Health Life's Greatest Prize Obtained By Eating Saxby's Pies'. The words on the card around the pig's neck would also raise eyebrows today: 'I Have A Hunch That When I Die They'll Put Me In A Saxby Pie'.

Right By the 1930s Saxby Brothers supplied pork butchers' and provision merchants' shops in most East Northamptonshire towns and villages. Two exceptions were Kettering and Rushden. In Kettering, the Lewin family, who are cousins to the Saxbys, had developed two very successful outlets; Ernest Lewin had worked in Saxby's original shop for a number of years. The founders' brother, George Saxby, ran the wonderful High Class Pork Butchers' shop in Rushden High Street featured in this pre-war photograph. This great little shop, with a very loyal set of customers, was run by George, then his son George junior, for some 80 years in total until George junior retired and Saxby Bros took it over. Both Lewins and George Saxby were very good customers, selling the full range of Saxby products. Sadly, all three shops are now closed.

Above The Saxby Directors have always been supporters of the industry's main Trade Associations, as well as always being ready for a good night out. In this picture, thought to be the London Provision Exchange Dinner in 1936, the Saxby contingent is on the table nearest to the camera. Facing us from the left are Herbert Saxby junior, Stan Collier, John Evans, Frank Saxby, and their brother Tom Saxby, who was the farmer of the family, farming in Great Doddington and later in Irchester.

Below A lighter moment, as 'Mother' Frank Saxby takes the piglet twins for a pram ride at Northampton Carnival in 1936. He is promoting the company's shop at 11 Abington St.

Saxby's had adopted the traditional parchment wrapper for pork pies many years before, and in 1937 the company joined in the celebrations for the Coronation of King George VI and Queen Elizabeth by introducing this special limited-edition pie wrapper, both sides of which are illustrated here.

In March 1939, war clouds were gathering over Europe, but in Wellingborough life was for the time being carrying on much as before. Saxby Bros won yet another prize, a Silver Medal for pork pies at the London Baking Trade Exhibition, as this handsome certificate shows.

A wonderful show of dummy pies fills the classic Ideal Home Exhibition stand of 1938. Note the 'We Recommend SAXBY'S' stickers on the wall; these were around for many years and are still much sought after. One in colour is featured on the title page.

The years encompassing the Second World War and the period of continued rationing and austerity that followed were a challenging time for Saxby's, just as they were for all the people and all the businesses of Britain.

For Saxby's the main issues during the war years were all about people and materials. They had to find enough skilled people to staff the factory, and this often meant asking women to do jobs that had traditionally been the preserve of the men who had gone off to war. Speaking many years later, Elsie Fleming, who went on to work for the company for more than 30 years, said of this time: 'I started in 1940 when my husband went to war. It was hard work, but everyone was very friendly, and I have stayed there ever since.'

Saxby's also had to find sufficient raw materials of the right price and quality to make the products. Talking about this period much later, Frank Saxby reflected that, 'Production was limited because of restrictions on pork, and during that period beef pies were the mainstay of our production, with only a few pork pies available. Some weeks during the war we had no allocation of meat at all, so to keep things going we made vegetable pies. These filled a gap, but of course they could not be compared with the pork pie.'

Other more practical matters, such as firewatching duties, got in the way of normal life too. The accounts for the year ended 31 January 1942 include: 'Expenditure on Air Raid precautions: Air Raid Shelter £255 15s 11d, Allowances to Firewatchers £57 15s 6d.'

SAXBY'S

BETTER FOOD PRODUCTS

JUST to remind you of the good old days and to assure that when normal times return, Saxby's will again offer many Cooked Meat Delicacies as previously unsurpassed for quality and flavour.

Saxby's Products are produced under the most Hygienic conditions in an extensive Model Factory and Bakery

SAXBY BROS., Ltd. *Telegrams: Saxby, Wellingborough Telephone: 2233 (3 Lines) Wellingborough* **Wellingborough and London**

SAXBY'S

REGISTER NOW for your Meat Supplies.

BEEF, MUTTON, LAMB and DAIRY FED PORK.

Full Ration Guaranteed.

Daily Deliveries to all Districts.

SAXBY'S

Wellingborough, 'Phone 2233 (3 lines).

RE-REGISTER AT

SAXBY'S

SPECIALISTS IN ALL RATIONED FOODS

OUR POLICY IS SERVICE, CIVILITY
AND A FAIR SHARE OF NON-RATIONED
FOODS AND ITEMS IN SHORT SUPPLY

NEXT WEEK'S SPECIAL OFFER:

Large Tins of Assorted SOUPS

2 for 1/4—Usually 1/9

SAXBY BROS. LTD.

GLOUCESTER PLACE and BRANCHES

WELLINGBOROUGH

Phone: 2233 (3 lines)

MAKERS OF THE FAMOUS "SAXBY" PIES

Now is the Time

you would usually be
thinking of a Delicious

SAXBY PIE

We hope to soon be
able to cope once
again with all orders
for our famous Pies
and Sausages.

SAXBY BROS. LTD.

WELLINGBOROUGH

Opposite left As well as the restrictions mentioned above, Saxby's had to cope within the constraints of the rationing rules. This leaflet, produced in 1945, reminds the reader of 'the good old days' and looks forward to 'when normal times return' and Saxby's can once again offer its full range of delicacies 'as previously unsurpassed for quality and flavour'. The company phone number is now 2233.

Opposite right All the meat that Saxby's was allowed to sell came on allocation, and rationing was of course very much the order of the day for everyone. This advert, placed in the *Evening Telegraph* in 1940, invites customers to register with Saxby's for their meat supplies. Saxby's shops continued to be busy throughout the war years.

Above Life had to go on, and rationing and competing with other retailers for customers' business resulted in adverts such as this. The company's advertised policy was 'Service, Civility, and Fair Share of Non-Rationed Foods and Items in Short Supply'.

Above right This advert, placed in *The Grocer* in November 1944, makes it clear that Saxby's pork pies would not be on the shopping list that Christmas, but, on a more positive note, the company looked forward to the return of normality.

Right The announcement in January 1945 by the Minister of Food that the official meat content of sausages was to be allowed to increase resulted in this advert, which appeared in the *Wellingborough News* on 2 February 1945.

"*.... the Sausage
can now look us in
the face*"

The Minister of Food in a
recent speech.

With the increase in
Meat Content (which the
Minister was referring to
above) you can now
expect an improvement
even in

Saxby's

SAUSAGES

SAXBY's

makers of the famous
Gold Medal

PORK PIES

invite your enquiries
as soon as the present
restriction of supplies
is lifted . . . . . .
In the meantime, note
these addresses for
future reference :—

Head Office and Bakery: **MELTON
WORKS, WELLINGBOROUGH**
Telephone : 2233 (3 lines)

London Office: **39a, Golders Way,
Golders Green, N.W.11**
Telephone : Speedwell 1045 (2 lines)

Left By June 1945 Saxby's felt able to advertise in *The Grocer* that its famous Gold Medal Pork Pies would be available again 'as soon as the present restriction of supplies is lifted'.

Below The war years gave the company a problem in recruiting sufficient staff. Despite many women taking on jobs in the factory previously regarded as the preserve of men, Saxby's was still short of workers. After the war, in 1947 according to the archive, the company's stand at the Wellingborough Trade Exhibition was used as what was effectively the company's first recorded recruitment campaign. The sign on the pie machine says 'Wholesale or Retail – The Food Trade offers Youth A Progressive Career'. And barely legible on the wall is: 'The Manufacture of Foods is Vital to this Country, and Offers an Interesting Career'.

Confusingly, also on the wall to the right is an acknowledgement of the company's half-century – 'Saxby's Have Been Making Good Foods For Fifty Years'. The company has either got its sums wrong or the archivist is wrong and the year is in fact 1954. The distinguished gentleman is Foreman Bill Lawrence once more.

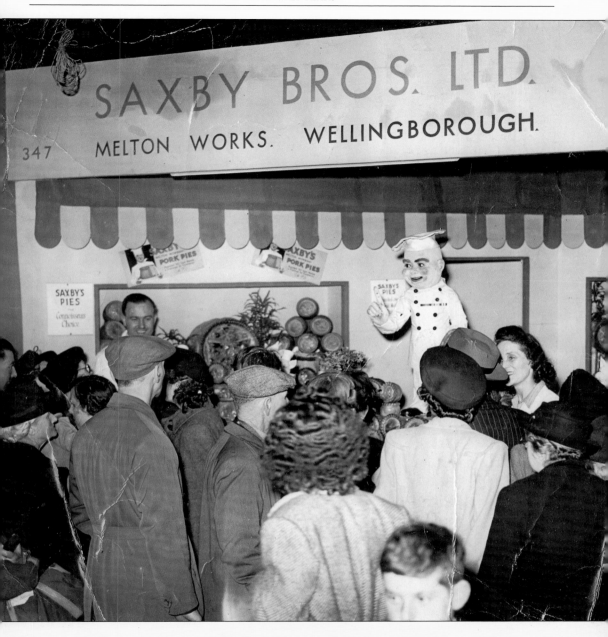

A visible sign that the war was over was the resumption of the Ideal Home Exhibition at Olympia, and this photo of the company's stand in 1948 shows that people's enthusiasm for Saxby's pies has definitely returned.

· 4 ·
The 1950s and 1960s
Austerity and expansion

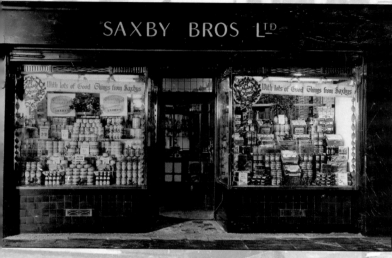

Left The early 1950s were still years of austerity, although there were still 'Lots of Good Things From Saxby's' in our Gloucester Place shop Christmas window display in 1951.

Below left These gentlemen were the team responsible for putting together the Ideal Home Exhibition stand in the early 1950s. They were, from the left, J. Bernie, L. Whittemore, G. Wood, Phil Panter, Frank Saxby, and R. Burton. Phil Panter continued to build the company's stands at shows, and much more, for the next 40 years.

Opposite The Saxby's stand at the 1952 Ideal Home Exhibition featured a working model of the pie factory. The pigs moved on a track from the farmyard and into Saxby's pie factory through the door on the left. Finished pork pies then simultaneously emerged from the door on the right, to be carried along the track straight into the Saxby's delivery lorry. Clever stuff! Sadly, this model has not survived.

Above Saxby's continued to supply all the London stores, and this is Selfridges' window display in 1952. Note the giant pork pie again, and the snazzy catchphrase 'Simple Simon meets Saxby's Pieman'. There is some inflation in prices now, and pork pies are selling for 3s 3d, 5 shillings, and 7 shillings.

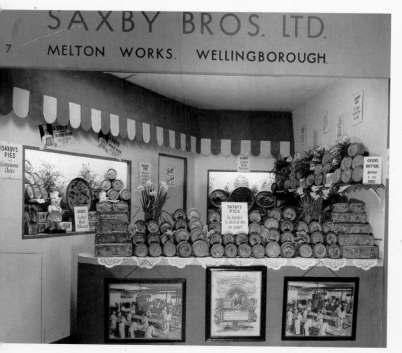

Left On the Ideal Home Exhibition stand in 1954 there is another wonderful display of pies, including the 20-pounder in the left-hand window. The poster to the left of the door says quietly 'Saxby's have been making Good Foods for Fifty Years'. Another states more assertively: 'SAXBY'S PIES The Standard by which all others are judged'.

Above Saxby's contribution to the celebrations for the Coronation of Queen Elizabeth II on 2 June 1953 was this magnificent decoration that adorned the front of the shop in Gloucester Place, Wellingborough. This picture is reproduced from an *Evening Telegraph* feature, and is a rare amateur colour photo, taken by the then manager of the Palace Cinema, which was situated on the opposite corner of the street.

Below The early 1950s also saw some notable landmarks at a family and company level. In January 1951 'the Guv'nor', as Herbert senior was affectionately known, enjoyed a special 80th birthday party with his family and members of staff at the Overstone Country Club. This photo shows him with his wife Ellen and sisters Chrissie and Lottie, and other family and staff around him.

Left Three years later the firm was 50 years old, and this event was celebrated in February 1955 with a dinner and dance, also at Overstone. Here the founders enjoy a moment before dinner with two of their longest serving colleagues: from the left, they are Tom Sewell senior, Herbert Saxby, Les Foster, and Ted Saxby.

Right Many photographs were taken that evening, and many long-service staff featured elsewhere can be spotted in this and the next picture – Charlie Platnauer, Len Pocock and Ron Coles, to mention but three.

Below The lady in the foreground is Hilda Bursnell, secretary to the Directors. Hilda was responsible for maintaining the company's archives during the 1950s and '60s, thus preserving many of the records in this book.

Top This series of photos of the bakehouse was taken in the mid-1950s. The first shows the top pie-makers, led by Bill Saxby senior on the left with Ron Coles next to him and Len Pocock opposite. All three of these gentlemen went on to serve 50 years with the firm. Bill Saxby had joined the company from school; a lovely character and story-teller, he was primarily responsible for the operation of the bakery, but he also looked after some important accounts, including Harrods and Fortnum & Mason, customers whom he always visited wearing his best suit and bowler hat.

Middle Len Pocock is adding the crimp finish to these 3lb pork pies. The wooden tables were wonderful for working with pastry – far better than the stainless steel that eventually replaced them. The ladies on the right are finishing off 1lb pies along the conveyor belt.

Bottom In another part of the bakehouse, 2lb pies are being finished off. All these pies are very much in the true traditional Melton Mowbray style, made with a coarse, un-cured pork meat and baked free-standing without the support of a tin or ring. More will be said about them later. In an interview in 1956, Frank Saxby gave a good indication of how the company viewed its business in the wider market when he said, 'Because the majority of our pies are still made by hand, we retain much of their character. Other pie manufacturers have turned completely to mechanisation – a thing that we have done only to a limited extent.'

Above left The smaller ½lb and 1lb pork pies were made on semi-automatic Camwheat pie machines, but still finished by hand. Once on baking trays, the pies are passed down the conveyor, after which they are given an egg wash spray before moving to the ovens.

Below left This line is making the 5oz pork pies, the 'tupp'ny pies'. The machine on the left presses out the pastry into the tin; the central station deposits the meat into the pie; and the machine on the right crimps the hand-placed lid.

Above This picture shows one of the wonderful draw-plate ovens, this time loaded with tins

containing just-roasted legs of pork. The trays of pies would be placed on the plate in the same way, then rolled back into the oven.

Below The London lorry is being loaded with 'SAXBY'S PIES' boxes by driver Arthur Barron outside the factory in 1958. The lorry, PRP 225, was an Albion. The factory frontage was the one that greeted both employees and visitors for many decades, having been extended forward from the original 1922 frontage some years before.

The company has always had a very active Sports and Social Club. The two events that members always most looked forward to were the Annual Dinner and Dance and the Annual Staff Outing.

These two pictures are of one of those fondly remembered outings – sailing down the river from Windsor on a Salter Bros pleasure boat in 1958. Nearly all the characters of the firm from that era are on one or other of the photos.

Almost 250 people were employed by Saxby's in 1958. At the time, club chairman Charlie Platnauer told the local paper, 'We are able to boast nearly 100% membership.' The club had been re-formed after the war, and members had their own club rooms in the billiard room at The Lindens. The subs were 3d per week.

For Saxby's, the arrival of the Ideal Home Exhibition in March always marked the coming out of winter and the transition into Easter and the busy spring and summer months. March 1959 was no exception, and a young John Saxby, son of Herbert junior, in the white coat, who had joined the company full-time in 1957, is rushed off his feet. Frank Saxby is serving on the right. Two familiar Saxby slogans are on display.

Right Saxby's shop in Gloucester Place, Wellingborough, was always regarded as the company's flagship store. Its Christmas displays were always impressive, this 1959 effort being typical.

Above The company regularly advertised in the trade press during these years, as it continued to build up its customer base, particularly in London and the Home Counties. This is the proof copy of an advert that appeared in *The Grocer* in September 1958. That slogan's there again!

Middle and right This exceptional decorated float won First Prize in the Wellingborough Carnival of 1959. Posing for the camera at the front of the float are Arthur Barron and Bill Lawrence. Another Saxby catchphrase appears on the side: 'For Goodness Sake Buy Saxby's'.

The rear of the float was just as impressive. At the picnic table are Sandra Hughes, Janet Corbyn and Pat Marshall. Notice the line 'We Live Well – We Buy Saxby's'. I agree!

Left Saxby's bakery worker Dick Thew hit the headlines in January 1960 when he beat the panel on the popular BBC TV show *What's My Line?*. His occupation? Hard Boiled Egg Sheller. He told the panel that during his time with Saxby's he had shelled hundreds of thousands of eggs. Today, of course, this job is performed entirely by machine.

Below left Ted Saxby shares a word with Frank Eaton, the Company Secretary for many years, on the occasion of the Sports and Social Club Dinner in 1960. Aged 86, Ted was the sole surviving founder now, Herbert having passed away in 1955. The same evening, he presented a gold watch to Fred Osman, manager of the company's St Albans branch, who had clocked up 30 years with the firm.

Ted's son, Bill Saxby senior, made the main speech that evening. He reviewed progress, stating that pie output had increased by 15%, with an extra 5 tons of pies and 100,000lb more sausages being made, and retail sales were up 20%. He said that while the firm's name was synonymous with good quality, our reputation was only gained through 'the excellent co-operation of the people who work with us'.

The ovens and bakehouse had been extensively altered four years before, and in his speech Mr Bill gave details of an imminent further expansion programme costing £30,000; a new abattoir and refrigeration plant, expanding capacity by 25%, would be complete by that Christmas.

Above right This was Saxby's stand at the Chamber of Trade Exhibition in 1961, featuring the acrobatic piggies circus act. Bill Lawrence is the gentleman on duty.

Inset This crossword, though perhaps not challenging *Times* crossword experts, did test the people of Wellingborough at that Chamber of Trade Exhibition in 1961. It was compiled by Mrs Betty Saxby. Have a go – no prizes, though!

Right John Saxby is the young man at the Wellingborough Chamber of Trade Exhibition in 1963. With him are Joyce Richardson, who worked in our Gloucester Place Delicatessen, and May Faulkner, from the Cambridge Street shop.

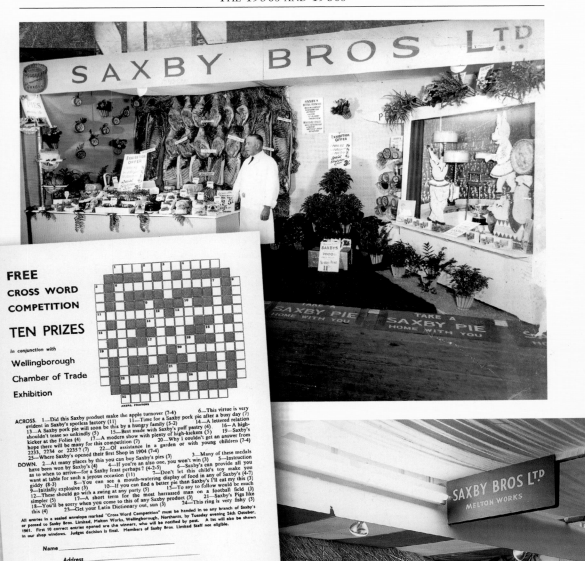

FREE CROSS WORD COMPETITION

TEN PRIZES

In conjunction with

Wellingborough

Chamber of Trade

Exhibition

ANKRO, PRINTERS

ACROSS. 1—Did this Saxby product make the apple turnover (7-4) evident in Saxby's spotless factory (11)   6—This virtue is very 13—A Saxby pork pie will soon be this by a hungry family (5-2)   11—Time for a Saxby pork pie after a busy day (7) shouldn't tease so unkindly (5)   15—Best made with Saxby's puff pastry (4)   14—A lettered relation kicker at the Folies (4)   17—A modern show with plenty of high-kickers (5)   16—A high-hope there will be many for this competition (7)   20—Why I couldn't get an answer from 2233, 2234 or 2235? (7)   22—Of assistance in a garden or with young children (7-4)   19—Saxby's 25—Where Saxby's opened their first Shop in 1904 (7-4)

DOWN. 2—At many places by this you can buy Saxby's pies (3)   3—Many of these medals have been won by Saxby's (4)   4—If you're an also one, you won't win (3)   5—Instruction as to when to arrive—for a Saxby feast perhaps ? (4-2-5)   6—Saxby's can provide all you giddy (8-3)   8—You can see a mouth-watering display of food in any of Saxby's (4-7)   want at table for such a joyous occasion (11)   7—Don't let this child's toy make you 9—Initially explosive (3)   10—If you can find a better pie than Saxby's I'll eat my this (3) 12—These should go with a swing at any party (5)   13—To say to follow would be much simpler (5)   17—A short term for the most harrassed man on a football field (3) 18—You'll be sorry when you come to this of any Saxby product (5)   21—Saxby's Pigs like this (4)   23—Get your Latin Dictionary out, sun (3)   24—This ring is very fishy (3)

All entries in a sealed envelope marked "Cross Word Compaction" must be handed in to any branch of Saxby's or posted to Saxby Bros. Limited, Melton Works, Wellingborough, Northants, by Tuesday evening 24th October, 1961. First 10 correct entries opened are the winners, who will be notified by post. A list will also be shown in our shop windows. Judges decision is final. Members of Saxby Bros. Limited Staff not eligible.

Name ....

Address ....

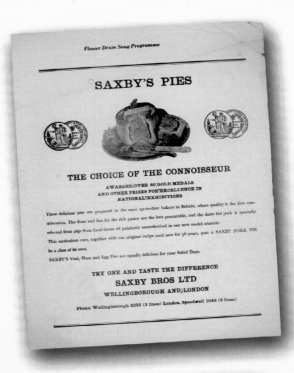

SAXBYS
MEAT PIES

Pork Pies 10d., 1/8, 3/3.
Individually made 3/6.
Veal/Ham/Egg 3/3,
or any weight cut 3/2 per lb.
Steak and Kidney Pies 2/6 or
3/3 each.

**Try one at Bentalls and
taste the difference.**

BARKERS
KENSINGTON

have recommended

SAXBYS
Melton Mowbray
PORK PIES
for over 40 years

*Made to an exclusive recipe from prime
young pork deliciously flavoured, encased
in rich pastry and then baked to a rich
golden brown.*

**TRY ONE TODAY —
THEN YOU WILL ORDER A
LARGE ONE FOR CHRISTMAS**

Above Trade with the London stores continued to blossom. This advert promoting SAXBYS MEAT PIES supported a feature on Bentalls of Kingston in the *Herald and News* in November 1960.

Above right This Christmas advert in the *Kensington News* of November 1964 celebrated more than 40 years of Barkers of Kensington selling Saxby's pork pies.

Below left In 1967 Saxby's retail shops still represented more than half the turnover of the company. The small market town of Thrapston at last got a permanent Saxby shop in December of that year, as this leaflet announced. Tuesday was cattle market day and this was always a day looked forward to by the Saxby pig buyer – usually in those days Mr Herbert. Though it was the smallest, and a glance at the opening hours explains why, Thrapston was always referred to, by Mr Herbert at least, as the Number One Shop.

Below right By 1969 the business was not only 65 years old, but was also celebrating 50 years of supplying its products to Messrs Harrods Ltd, and this advert in Harrods' *Wine and Food Magazine* records the fact.

Back at the factory, production was continuing to increase, and, earlier in 1969, we had opened our new despatch extension, our third major development on the site.

SAXBYS - -
Have at last acquired Permanent
Premises in

THRAPSTON
40 HIGH STREET
This very modern shop will be
opened on

FRIDAY, 8th DECEMBER, 1967 at
9 a.m.

with many special offers; a few
of these are detailed over-leaf.

The Directors would like to
thank all customers for their
loyal support over the years,
often under difficult conditions,
and hope for their continued
support at the New Premises.

Hours of business:— TUESDAY, WEDNESDAY and
FRIDAY   9 a.m.-5.30 p.m.
SATURDAY   9 a.m.-1 p.m.

Have a SAXBY pie for Christmas

AWARDED OVER 100 GOLD MEDALS AND OTHER PRIZES IN NATIONAL EXHIBITIONS

These delicious pork pies are prepared in Britain's most modern and hygienic bakery in the heart of the Midlands, where quality is the first consideration. The flour and fats for the rich pastry are the best procurable, the succulent pork is specially selected from local farms, and the pigs are painlessly anaesthetised in the new model abattoir.

Meticulous care, together with their original recipe, used now for 65 years, puts a Saxby Pie in a class of its own.

Saxbys are proud that for 50 years they have supplied Messrs Harrods Ltd. Again they will make a special Christmas feature of Saxbys Pies, available in 1 lb., 2 lb. and 3 lb. sizes in Pork or Veal, Ham and Egg.

ORDER ONE EARLY

SAXBY BROS LTD, WELLINGBOROUGH
LONDON AREA OFFICE OSA 7-52570

Above John Saxby and Jim Saxby were made Directors in 1966, and they, together with Michael Bell (grandson of Ted Saxby, *far right*) and myself (*second from right*) were now taking a much more active involvement in the business. I had started in 1968 and, after a period of work experience in Australia, served an apprenticeship in the butchery department, where I became an expert in the art of making black puddings. John changed roles to take charge of the family's farming interests in 1974, though he remained a Director. Michael and I were appointed to the Board in 1977, and these portraits were taken in 1979. The family tree on page 96 shows how we all fit into the family.

Below By 1973 I had progressed to the bakehouse. In this photo, myself and Bill Green, our top pie-maker for many years, look on knowledgably as Len Pocock checks to see that this special 8lb pork pie has been properly baked.

Len had joined the business, aged 14, in 1935, and from the start he involved himself in as many different jobs as he could. He remembers one of his early tasks: 'We used to make horseradish cream in a room upstairs. I had to go up to the local dairy to fetch the milk. We also made Christmas puddings, and I was sent up the road to the Red Lion to bring back the stout! My first wage was 10 shillings a week. We used to work very long hours and didn't get paid overtime, but it was enjoyable and everyone helped each other.'

Len was foreman and general fixer by now, having come through the ranks to take over from Tom Sewell on his retirement in 1967. He was a huge asset to the business right up to his retirement in 1985, clocking up approaching 50 years' service.

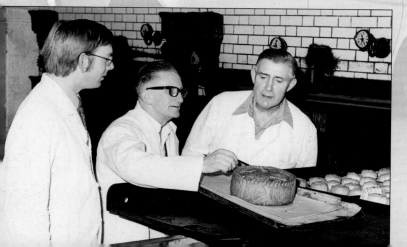

Right We exhibited at the Peterborough Show in 1972. Our 'This Little Pig Went To SAXBY'S' animated model always entertained the audience. Sides of smoked English bacon and a row of York hams created a delicious aroma. Decimalisation had arrived in 1971 and 1lb pork pies were now 22p each.

Below The shop management group held annual meetings to review performance and there was usually an opportunity for a photo-call on the terrace of Wyvill, Frank Saxby's house next to the factory. This is the shop managers' line-up in 1974, and a pretty formidable team they were: back row, Mike Bell, Jim Saxby and Brian Wells (Bedford); middle row, Frank Saxby, Anthony Saxby, Ted Oswick (Northampton), Charlie Jarvis (Abington Square, Northampton), Fred Bowman (Dunstable), Ken Scott (Cambridge Street, Wellingborough), Bill Saxby senior, John Saxby and Phil Stapleton (factory stores); front row, Alan Foster (Finance Director), Fred Osman (St Albans), Charlie Platnauer (factory stores), Edgar Watson (Midland Road, Wellingborough), Vic Rowlands (Luton), Harold Ransom (Gloucester Place, Wellingborough) and Derek Dickinson (Harpenden).

Above This 1975 photograph of the Saxby van and lorry fleet lined up in front of what were then still the main offices reflects a transition period in the company's development. It was a more modern fleet of mostly Ford Transit vans, but most were still un-refrigerated. We had updated the company logo with the script-style '*Saxby's*' that was the standard for a while on packaging and advertising material during the 1970s.

Below The 1970s were a testing period for the company in many ways. The economy was struggling to cope with very high inflation, high wage increases, and high interest rates. Investment was difficult to fund. For Saxby's, it was a time of steady growth and planning for future expansion. These photos of the abattoir, butchery and sausage departments in around 1975 preceded a major factory development that would see all these rooms disappear.

This is the abattoir in the mid-1970s. Around 120 pigs a day, sourced from 11 local markets and direct from farmers, were being slaughtered. Bill Hooper and Brian Dunkley are two of the slaughtermen.

Above In this photo, Jim Saxby (in the trilby hat) presides over the butchery area. Peter Frost, on the right, was in charge of the sausage department for many years. The boning process was a simple system that worked for us. The carcases were divided into three: the loins were cut out for the Saxby shops trade, the legs were boned and tied for roasting, and the shoulders and bellies went into the pies and sausages.

Below The sausage girls, using fairly basic equipment, link sausages in natural casings; the drier is in the background. Sausages were the company's second largest product category, after pork pies. The lady in the foreground is Val Coode.

Left Didn't we do well? In October 1977 we had some fun when Saxby's was invited to participate in the very first series of *The Generation Game* with Bruce Forsyth. Bill Green was the master craftsman who did the demonstration and Bill Saxby was the judge. This window display at Gloucester Place ensured that everyone in Wellingborough knew about it! In the foreground is each stage of the production of a 2lb pork pie.

Below Bill Green rehearses the process of forming the pastry round the block; and Bill Saxby rehearses the judging – definitely 10 out of 10!

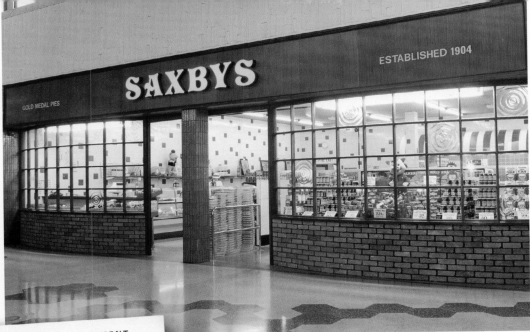

Good news or bad news? The decision had been taken in 1976 by Wellingborough Council to demolish a great swathe of old Wellingborough to make way for that wonderful new style of shopping, the Arndale Centre. This caused a great deal of anguish for the Saxby Board as we debated whether or not we too should join this modern retailing trend. In the end we did, as this 'sad announcement' explains. For the first time, non-perishables would be self-service from shelves, and 'Payment will be by quick service check-outs'. Whatever would they think of next?

The new store opened on 18 April 1978, and the sad news was that this meant the final closure, three days earlier, of our original branch in Midland Road after 74 years of trading. The good news was that the new store was a great success from the start – Mr Harold Ransom and the rest of the staff saw to that. Margaret Moore and Pauline Watts are two of the ladies seen here in the shop with Harold.

75 years of progress
1904-1979

Saxby's Product Range

Melton Mowbray Pies
Pork Pies: 5/6 oz., 9/10 oz., 1 lb, 1½ lb, 2 lb, 3 lb; Pork Galas, Ham & Egg Galas (Average weight 6½ lb) Ham & Egg 1 lb, Ham & Chicken 1 lb, Ham & Chicken (Round) 6 lb.

Pies for heating
3 sizes of Steak & Kidney, Cornish Pasties, Chicken & Ham Flans, Pizza Pies.

Sausage and Cooked Meats
Sausages—Pork (8 to lb), Pork Chipolatas, Pork and Beef, and Sausage Meat.
Cooked Meats—Roasted Legs of Pork, Cooked Gammons, Hams-on-the-bone, Haslet, Polony, Black Pudding etc.

Sundries
Sausage Rolls, pre-packed Short and Puff Pastry, Gold Medal Christmas Puddings.

Above left In 1979 Saxby's celebrated its 75th anniversary, and the front cover of the anniversary brochure featured an ample display of Melton Mowbray pork pies, still the mainstay of the company's production. Presenting the pie is Jean Burgess, second in command to Harold Ransom in the new Arndale Centre shop.

Inside the brochure is a shot showing most of the product range at that time. The only slicing pie, apart from the galas, was the 6lb ham and chicken pie. Twenty years later there would be more than 30 different varieties and sizes of this type of pie.

Left The factory was gradually becoming at least a little more automated. This was our first in-line pie machine, making small 5/6oz pork pies, pictured in 1979. In the background are rows of empty pie runners waiting to be filled.

Above In 1979 the factory site looked very different from today. The terraced houses in Brook Street East (top left corner) were soon to be demolished to create space for what is now the meat prep area; the main offices and factory frontage were still much as they had been for the previous 40 years; and the lairage (back right) and paddock, and abattoir of course, were still operating.

The Ideal Home Exhibition 1970s and 1980s

Above Every year the Ideal Home Exhibition attracted celebrity visitors, who often visited our stand. Here are a few memorable Saxby moments from the 1970s and '80s, starting with The Queen Mother, who officially opened the show in 1978 and who stopped on her tour round for a chat about the merits of Saxby's pies. I was fortunate enough to be the Saxby person on duty that day.

Left Sometimes we had good news to publicise. In 1972 we won another First Prize, this time at the British Baker Exhibition in London. The news dramatically reached our stand by telegram: 'SAXBYS PIES AWARDED FIRST PRIZE ... CONGRATULATIONS' was the message.

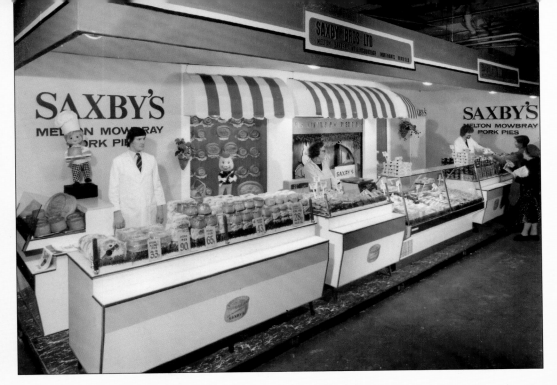

Above In 1976 an IRA bomb went off inside Olympia, and the stand immediately in front of ours took the full blast. Mr Frank Saxby, on duty with Mike Bell and my brother Michael that day, said afterwards, 'We were quite close but did not suffer any ill effects. A big show of dummy pies and two animated displays were wrecked, but none of us was hurt. It was very distressing.' Eighty-five people were injured.

Below Jon Pertwee signs an autograph in 1977. The Union Jacks on the wall in the background are celebrating the Royal Silver Jubilee.

Left The iconic June Whitfield was a regular visitor, here sharing a joke with Frank Saxby, also in 1977. Could it be about the 'Piggy Express' – 'I hope we'll be good enough for Saxby's!'

Below left In 1981 Paul Daniels tries to do a disappearing trick with a basket of pies, but Mike Bell hangs on grimly.

The stand gradually evolved during this period, but in this photograph of the 1985 stand, the pie display is still completely un-refrigerated. In charge that day was a young Chris Saunders, on the left, with Lawrence Lane next to him, and 1lb pork pies are now 99p. Our last Ideal Home Exhibition was in 1989.

· 6 ·
The 1980s
A positive decade

Below The 1980s was a very busy and positive decade for the company. New sales opportunities were opening up, a major factory expansion was being planned, our

marketing function was starting to operate strongly, and our product packaging and presentation were being sharpened up.

Nonetheless, this composed photograph of the traditional Saxby pork pie confirmed where Saxby's prime focus still continued to lie. It was taken by Hussman's, the refrigeration people, for a trade advert after they had completed an overhaul of our refrigeration system in 1981.

Below All but three of the management team looking after the factory in 1980 were gold watch people with, by definition, years of experience. Here they are on the steps at Wyvill: Frank Saxby, Jim Saxby, Anthony Saxby, Mike Bell, Alan Boag, Bill Brown, Harry Ayres, Charles Southcombe, Colin Smith, David Taylor, Brian Dunkley, Doreen Parker, Len Pocock and Bryan Martin.

Above The refrigeration overhaul was part of a major redevelopment of the butchery section of the factory. Much of the old butchery was dismantled, and the terraced houses on the factory side of Brook Street East were demolished to make room for our new butchery hall, chillers and freezers. Here, in 1981, this work is getting under way.

Below The wedding of Prince Charles and Lady Diana Spencer took place on 29 July 1981, and following the precedent of Charles's grandmother's wedding celebrations, when we had brought out a celebration pie, Saxby's launched a special limited edition Royal Wedding Souvenir pork pie, using this wrapper, and put on a special display in the Arndale Centre shop window. We even made a three-tiered Royal Wedding pork pie.

Saxby's continued to exhibit at various Agricultural Shows throughout the 1980s. This photograph, of the May 1982 stand at the Herts Show, features two Saxby stalwarts doing their bit – George Saxby, serving, having recently retired from his Rushden shop, and John Mereweather, Finance Director and general good man, adding up to the left of picture. This was a time of high inflation: 1lb pork pies were now 85p, our prices having risen an astonishing 13 times in three years. The 1lb pie had been 60p in February 1979.

Below left In the 1980s pig procurement was still a significant task for the Directors, who were required to visit the livestock markets every day. In early December, when the Royal Smithfield Show was on, this was especially the case. In 1982, for instance, we purchased the Supreme Champion pen of pigs, the Reserve Champion, two Class Champions, and scores of other prize-winners. These are some of the prize-winning pigs outside the Saxby lairage, with pig buyer Jim Saxby and shop manager Harold Ransom.

Below right Each winner came with a full-colour certificate, and these, together with some of the pork carcases, are here displayed in the Gloucester Place shop window. Saxby's liked to claim that every pie at Christmas contained prize-winning pork, and in 1982 this could almost have been the case!

One of many remarkable Saxby servants is Frank Skelton. His story began in 1933 when, as an 18-year-old, he started work as a salesman for Saxby's in the Hertfordshire area. He tells the story of targeting Welwyn Department Store as a customer, and riding his motorbike and sidecar to the store carrying tasty samples. He must have been successful, because a week later he was given a lift to the store by Muriel Saxby, daughter of founder Ted Saxby, with a hamper full of pork pies ready for sale. For a time after this, their order was sent from Wellingborough to Luton by train, then on to Welwyn Garden City on a branch line, long since closed. Shortly after, Frank learned to drive, and from then on he delivered the pies to the store by van.

Frank carried on selling Saxby's pies to customers throughout Hertfordshire for the next 50 years. A great character, his last job was to help set up an exhibition at Welwyn Department Store celebrating the 50th anniversary of his first delivery. Pictured with Frank in the store in May 1983 are store manager Paul Wren and Bunny Warren, another Saxby stalwart who was from our St Albans shop.

Part of the Welwyn Department Store celebrations was a magnificent three-tiered pie inscribed '50 YRS / W D S / SAXBYS'. It was the subject of a 'guess-the-weight' competition; unfortunately the actual weight has not been recorded...

Burglar trapped

POLICE caught a burglar in the early hours of Friday morning in bizarre circumstances that might merit an entry in Stephen Pile's "Book of Heroic Failures".

Attempting to break into Saxby's the Silver Street butchers via a skylight in the roof he slipped and fell.

He was later found by police calling for assistance, trapped and wedged between a generator and some iron bars.

He was extricated with some difficulty and taken to the police station where he is helping police with their enquiries.

An extract from *Bedfordshire on Sunday*, 19 August 1984...

Melton Mowbray pork pies

This 1986 Pork Pie Month campaign shelf 'wobbler' promoted Saxby's Melton Mowbray pork pies to our customers throughout the UK. The basic wrapper design is one with which long-standing fans will be familiar.

This provides an opportunity to expand on Melton Mowbray pork pies, which have been referred to many times throughout this story, and are very much a common denominator throughout our first 100 years.

So, why Melton Mowbray? Well, it is a style of pork pie that has its roots in Melton Mowbray and the East Midlands region, dating back to the 19th and early 20th centuries. The connection was with the strong farming and, more particularly, cheese-making tradition in the area. A by-product of cheese production is whey, and this was used by farmers as an important component in the dietary intake of the substantial local pig population. This meant that a particularly large quantity of 'dairy-fed' pork was available, and this in turn led to many pork butchers in every East Midlands town developing their own Melton Mowbray pork pies.

The traditional characteristics of such pies are that they are made with natural pork, chopped fairly coarsely and with seasoning added. They are not made with cured pork. This means that the cooked pie meat will be typically 'porky' in colour, rather than pink. The pie will also be free-standing when baked, giving it the bow-sided shape that is another vital characteristic.

All the pictures of pie-making throughout this book demonstrate Saxby's adherence to these principles. In fact, we have carried the flag for Melton Mowbray pies for a long period, especially in the late 1950s and 1960s when there were very few manufacturers remaining. It is pleasing that other manufacturers have in recent years resumed commercial

production. An Association of Melton Mowbray Pork Pie Makers has recently been formed, of which Saxby's is a member, and it is possible that in time the above definition, together with a requirement that the product is made within a defined area of the East Midlands, will become protected by European law from 'mere imitations'.

In 1985 the Saxby trading business was broadly split into three categories. One was the 14 Saxby shops, which were at their peak. They still sold a terrific amount of our own products, especially of course the pork pies. But the signs were definitely there that future growth was likely to be difficult for our style of retail outlet as shopping habits changed and supermarkets continued to expand. Our trade with the supermarkets was becoming more and more significant; sales of existing lines were growing considerably, and development opportunities were beginning to appear in other areas.

Our direct deliveries to retailers also continued. We had delivery routes through the Midlands and Home Counties, up to the North East, and down into the South West. However, it was clear to the company that many of our independent customers were now finding life very tough, and many more had already ceased trading.

Much of our distribution to the independent trade was through our network of distributors and agents. Our distributor structure was thriving, covering parts of Scotland and South Wales as well as most of England, as this Saxby's service map from a 1985 brochure illustrates. Each and every letter represents a valued distributor, many of whom had acted as our agents in their area for many years. Without them we would not have been able to grow the business in the way we did during that period.

Notice the photo of the van in the illustration. By 1985 our van fleet was dressed in a new Royal Blue livery, and the vehicles were now refrigerated as standard. This Ford Transit box-van had the honour of being the first to show off our newly acquired SAX 8Y number plate – a customer in Cardiff had tipped us off that this might be available. Naturally, we won the Best In Class prize at that year's Cherished Number Plate Rally. The number is still going strong today, and is now on its fourth vehicle.

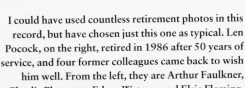

KEY
DISTRIBUTION AREAS

◉ Indicates main town or city with retail outlets supplied direct from Wellingborough (■)

A	Edinburgh Distributor	I	Oxford Agency
B	Glasgow Distributor	J	London Area Agencies & Direct
C	Cleveland Agency	K	Luton Agency
D	Manchester Agency	L	Stowmarket Agency
E	Hull Agency	M	Bournemouth Agency
F	South Wales Agency	N	Brighton Agency
G	Cheltenham Depot	O	Kent Agencies
H	Bristol Depot		

I could have used countless retirement photos in this record, but have chosen just this one as typical. Len Pocock, on the right, retired in 1986 after 50 years of service, and four former colleagues came back to wish him well. From the left, they are Arthur Faulkner, Charlie Platnauer, Edgar Watson, and Elsie Fleming. All four had done more than their share for Saxby's in their many years with us.

Above Saxby's marketing approach may not have been very sophisticated, but the company excelled at in-store demonstrations. Our team of youth and experience in 1987 was Len Binley, a master baker and pie-maker with decades of experience, and Tim Charles, our then Development Manager. They were in great demand for pie-making demonstrations, and visited many top stores, including Harrods and Rackhams.

Above and right Throughout the 1980s Saxby's supported its distributors and agents by exhibiting at the various food trade shows. This was the company's stand at the Chilled Food Fair at the NEC in 1987...

...and this was the same show two years later, when we were proudly celebrating '85 years of Excellence'. Sales Director Mike Bell 'cuts the cake' with Anthony Saxby.

We enjoyed good export sales during this period, specialising in countries with plenty of 'ex-pat' Brits, such as Bermuda, Bahrain, Gibraltar and Hong Kong. We supplied the Bull and Bear Pub in Central Hong Kong with pies and sausages, whose in-house advert tells us that we were a hit with at least one customer: '"Saxby satisfies" says Cyn.' We also supplied Hong Kong retailers Oliver's, Park'N Shop, and Wellcome.

By the mid-1980s it was clear to the Directors that another major decision point in the company's development had been reached. While the independent trade, including Saxby's shops, was increasingly feeling the squeeze from competition from the multiple retailers, those very supermarkets were offering us opportunities to grow into new areas. To take advantage of this we needed to invest on two fronts – first, simply to give ourselves the capacity to meet the expected volumes, and second, to ensure that the factory standards of hygiene and control remained at the very highest level now expected as the norm by our customers and by ourselves.

This resulted in the decision to invest £5m in developing the site on all four sides over a two-year build period. Significantly, the abattoir closed in 1985 as the first stage in this development, bringing to an end more than 70 years of operating our own slaughtering facility. Here the very last batch of pigs is taken to the holding pens by Richard Bolton, watched by Frank Saxby, head slaughterman Jim Askew, Jim Saxby and Don Smith, the factory manager. The family had mixed feelings on the day, but I think we all knew it was the right decision.

Opposite This new development resulted in a complete re-organisation of the meat receiving and preparation areas at the heart of the factory (*top*). We also built new ovens and jellying facilities, new laboratories and product development areas, and a new dedicated wrapping and despatch area. All this meant that the 60-year-old offices had to go very early in the project, and in the second photograph the new jellying and pie-cooling areas are being constructed in front of the old façade. For almost three years we managed in very basic Portakabin offices in the yard.

Above The new office block was the last building to be completed, and we eventually moved in early in 1988.

Right Behind it was the new pastry-making factory known affectionately as 'N' Block, inside which we see part of the new pastry wrapping line, illustrating the standard of finish that was now typical throughout the factory. On the line are Pam Mitchell and Barbara West.

Royal visit: Princess Diana opens the new factory

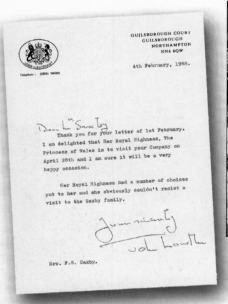

Above By the end of 1987, after three years and more than £5m of expenditure, all the disruption and dust and confusion was coming to an end. The excellent new facilities were coming on stream, and the completion date was in sight. All we needed now was someone to officially open the new factory. But who could we get?

Could we possibly get a member of the Royal Family? Our first choice was Princess Diana, and in October 1987 we wrote to John Lowther, then Lord Lieutenant for Northamptonshire, the contact in these matters, with our request. He wrote back not very optimistically saying,

'I rather doubt the Princess of Wales will be available but will keep my options open.' We heard nothing for four months, then out of the blue in February 1988 came this letter, and suddenly it was all 'action stations'.

Above A massive amount of logistics and planning went into the next three months, masterminded by our great organiser, John Mereweather. The whole workforce became involved, and were brought together for this photo-call early in April 1988. The management team on the front row, from the left, are Karen King, Alan Hancock, John Hare, Jim Saxby, Don Smith, Frank Saxby, Anthony Saxby, John Mereweather, Brian Dunkley, Peter Black, David Hewitt, Doreen Parker and Charles Southcombe.

Opposite bottom All too quickly, 28 April arrived, together with hundreds of employees, retired employees, local schoolchildren, a school orchestra, invited guests, and police, all ready to welcome the Princess. In the welcoming party, being introduced to Her Royal Highness by Lord Lieutenant John Lowther, are a very proud Chairman Frank Saxby and Joint Managing Directors Jim and Anthony Saxby. Also in the line up are the Mayor, Councillor Roy Blackmore, Peter Fry MP, and other dignitaries.

This page The Princess enjoyed a tour of the factory, guided by Jim Saxby and factory manager Don Smith. She was shown how to make a traditional Melton Mowbray pork pie (*right*) by master craftsman Sid Wallis, hidden behind HRH, assisted by Tim Charles. Jim Saxby adds words of encouragement. She then had a go herself, and enjoyed a good chat with Sid (*bottom right*). Notice the wooden pie blocks, the same ones that featured in the 1922 bakery photo on page 16. We were in trouble for not insisting that she remove her engagement ring, and for not making her wear a hair-net. Well, would you have done?

Above and right In the packing room the Princess talked with Mary Salter and a colleague on the hand wrapping line, then later, in slightly pensive mood, she listened to my speech of welcome.

Below After my few words, she unveiled this fine slate plaque in front of many staff and guests. We gave her two hand-painted model Saxby vans, in 1920s livery, for William and Harry. The plaque still has pride of place in our main office reception today.

Below The Princess was a wonderful Guest of Honour. She was lovely, of course, and so interested in all the people she met. She even tried the products – away from the cameras – which she clearly enjoyed. Here she finishes her tour with a 'walkabout' among the crowd. Her three hours with us went all too quickly, but we continued to celebrate with the staff at a party long into the evening. It was quite a day!

Princess Diana's visit was effectively Sid Wallis's swansong. He retired in October 1988 after 50 years' service. Our chief competition pie-maker for 30 years, Sid is seen here with Sales Manager Roy Hugh in 1983, celebrating another victory, this time the Institute of Meat Challenge Trophy at the East of England Show. Some of our other cups, trophies and medals are also displayed.

Sid's had been a fascinating and rewarding career. He joined Saxby's in 1938, aged 14. He already had a job, engineering sewing machines, but decided to move when he was offered an extra 2 shillings a week. His first job was egging up the 'tupp'ny pies' before the lid was put on by a skilled craftsman. His ambition was to become a master craftsman himself, and he realised that to achieve this he had to take every opportunity to 'get on the board' and learn this craftwork. He practised crimping the pie lids whenever he could. He remembers very long hours, but found it a 'brilliant place to work. Jobs were easy to get, but I decided to stay.' He well remembers 'the Guv'nor', Herbert senior, coming round, poking him with his stick when he was cleaning and telling him sternly to sweep all the way under the table!

Called up into the Navy in 1942, Sid served in the North Atlantic and elsewhere, eventually coming home to Britain from Philadelphia on the *Queen Mary*. Returning to Saxby's, Sid found it difficult to settle, but was given the opportunity to take over the Pastry Department when the incumbent, Tommy Attwell, retired. He went on to become one of the leading experts in pie pastry, and competition pies, in the country. He took over responsibility for the latter from Tom Sewell, from whom he had learned so much, and for the next 35 years made all the company's competition entries, winning dozens of medals and diplomas along the way.

Pastry mixing was hard work, especially in the early days when the 140lb flour sacks had to be stacked three high in the store. He had to go up and down the vertical ladder joining the flour store with the mixing area dozens of times a day, then the finished pastry all had to be removed from the Artofex mixing bowl into troughs by hand.

Sid was also responsible for much of the company's product development in the early days. He felt there was a demand for short pastry, and in 1963 he developed a recipe using Australian flour, based on one he'd brought back from the Navy. It first appeared on our price list at Christmas that year, when the retail price was 1s 6d (see page 52). He remembers Bill Saxby senior saying to him, 'You'll never sell it, boy.' But of course it quickly took off and soon sales matched those of its illustrious predecessor, puff pastry. Today, it remains one of our best-selling lines.

A changing world, yet a world that continues just the same: our look at the 1990s begins with a Gold Watch day. It has always been the firm's tradition to recognise long service with a gift, and in 1990 there were seven people who had reached that landmark. Here, having just received their watches from Jim Saxby and Frank Saxby, are Eric Coles, Phil Stapleton, Stan May, Lena Clemenzi, Zophie Benderz, June Rowland and Pam Mitchell. Phil Stapleton, who was Stores Manager and went on to complete 33 years of service before he retired in 1998, was the 100th person to receive a Long Service Award. The latest recipient, Chris Saunders in 2003, was number 136. All 136 are listed in Appendix 1 on pages 94-5.

CRABS   LOBSTERS   SAXBY'S
GOLD MEDAL
MELTON
MOWBRAY
PORK
PIES   OAK
SMOKED
LOCH FYNE
KIPPERS

Above This fishmonger's shop in Cirencester had been, in many ways, a typical Saxby customer, but by the 1990s this was no longer the case. Saxby's has always had the knack of keeping up with the changing world, and never has that been more important than in the last decade. Traditional small independent retailers such as the fishmonger had been the backbone of our business, selling our Melton Mowbray pork pies up and down the country, and serviced by our nationwide network of distributors. By 1991 a new era was dawning. While we continued to service the independents, we had also to respond to the development opportunities being offered by the multiples. As Mike Bell, Sales Director, said in an interview at the time, 'We are now committed to supplying major multiples with our products. We have put in a lot of investment to cater for their needs. We have made considerable investments to enable us to cope efficiently and economically with the increased volume, while retaining our flexibility and, above all, the quality that has made us famous.' The multiples now represented more than half of our business, and it was clear that this must increase.

Right By 1993 our slicing pie range was expanding fast and new varieties were being devised almost weekly to satisfy our customers' needs for unique product offerings for their delicatessen counters. The products in this promotional photo were all sold under the Saxby name – and indeed quite a few still are.

We had been exhibiting at the East of England Show since the early 1970s, our stall was always popular, and sales brisk. However, by 1993 it was starting to become harder to justify the time and effort that was required.

It was, though, always great fun and was a chance for the sales team to have a go at proper selling to real customers. In this line-up at the 1993 show (*middle*) are, from the left, Jo Bell, Chris Saunders, Dennis Bridge, Danny Miles-Davies, Ian White, Malcolm Lupson, Mike Turner, Michael Bell and Paul Jackson.

And just to show it wasn't all boys, here are the girls (*bottom*): Karen King, Technical Manager, with Sandra Stephenson and Joanna Dunkley, also in 1993. We carried on exhibiting at the East of England for just one more year.

Right The demise of the small retailer was a fate also awaiting Saxby's shops. In July 1994 the company announced that it was to close four of its last remaining five retail outlets. Here are the frontage and interior of our Northampton shop in Mercers Row – a cracking store full of interest, but it just could not take enough money. Our press release explained: 'We know our stores have been valued by our loyal Saxby customers for many years. However, the huge growth of the big multiples has made our shops less and less competitive.' We received many letters from upset customers: 'Saxby's is one of the oldest and best shops of its kind in Northampton. What a shame so many of these shops are going, never to return.' 'I was horrified to learn that Saxby's is to close its Thrapston shop. They have been in the town for many years and have an excellent reputation and good quality food. Can nothing be done?' Of course, nothing could be done. It was nice to receive these comments, but sad for all of us that these shops had to close.

Below The Saxby Sports and Social Club continued actively throughout the 1990s. In this photograph three Saxby old stagers, Jean Wood, May Mabbutt and Pauline Martin, have been part of a team pedalling around the Silverstone circuit in October 1993, with Anthony Saxby, helping to raise funds for the Boys Clubs of Northamptonshire.

Top These photographs, taken in February 1994, show that despite all the advances the business has made, some things remain much as before. This trusty old pie machine, a Camwheat, was by now itself more than 50 years old, but still made the best pork pies, and we still had two on the go full time. Sadly, they only come out on special occasions now. The lady handling the pie is Kath Page.

Middle This is the same room as in that earlier picture of the bakery in 1922 (page 16). By 1994, however, more or less the whole room was dedicated to the large cutting pies, both round and gala. Unlike other areas of the factory, the pie lines were still very labour-intensive. These pies were now sold through most major multiple supermarkets in their deli departments, many produced to special recipes according to the customer's particular requirements. This new growth was more than compensating for lost sales elsewhere.

Bottom Saxby's of the 1990s offered careers in many different specialisations – not just manufacturing, human resources (as personnel was now called), sales and finance, but also marketing, product development and technical departments, all now well established. Jacqueline Class was our senior food micro-biologist.

Right Frank Saxby died on 30 March 1995. He had joined the company in 1928, and apart from his years of war service worked for us right up to the day he died, aged 86. He was a great leader of the business and was instrumental in much of the progress made during the 1960s and '70s, and beyond. He always loved 'checking up' on the shops. He is seen here admiring the display in the newly refurbished Swansgate shop in 1993.

Below In January 1995 the company announced that Bill Saxby had joined the Board, and that Paul Massey, Karen King, Peter Black and Steve Macro had been appointed Divisional Directors. Together with myself and Mike Bell, this was the team (photographed here without Bill Saxby) that was tasked by the shareholders to take the business forward towards the new millennium. Announcing the appointments and the creation of the company's Executive Management Group, Chairman Jim Saxby said, 'Business with the multiples has risen and our foodservice division under the Irchester Grange brand continues to grow. Saxby's is now in excellent shape to tackle the challenge of the years to come.'

Below Christmas has always been, and still is, a frantic time at Saxby's. In December 1995 Bill Saxby was persuaded to pose for this newspaper feature. It was to be another record Christmas, and Bill estimated for the article sales of 50,000 Melton Mowbray pies, more than a million packets of pastry, and 100 tonnes of Christmas puddings. 'We're very busy; it's a traditional Saxby Christmas – another record-breaker.'

■ **COMPANY NEWS**

Saxby's expand

Saxby Bros Ltd., the family run firm of food manufacturers, has announced a record year for 1994 together with details of a new executive management team.

Chairman, Jim Saxby, is delighted with the 20% increase on last year. He said: "1994 has seen solid achievements in key areas. Business with the multiples has risen and our foodservice division continues to grow. Our distributors serving the independent sector also had a record year, and we are beginning to see very encouraging results from Europe.

"We have recently completed a £6M investment programme at our EEC approved Wellingborough factory. I am particularly pleased to announce four new divisional directors: Paul Massey, divisional director, sales & marketing; Peter Black, divisional director, operations; Karen King, divisional director, technical; Stephen Macro, divisional director of finance.

"The main board has also been strengthened by the addition of Bill Saxby, the first of the fourth generation of Saxbys.

"We have excellent facilities, a loyal and committed team, and a priceless heritage. And I am expecting 1995 to be even better."

Saxby's have a new heavyweight team at the top.

to on as

es all ve

off 's, ss to

he to

■ **SLICE OF THE ACTION** . . . director Bill Saxby sees another pork pie consignment on its way

ET picture: CDC49424

Top John Mereweather was our finance director for some 18 years. He retired in July 1996, but continued to be involved with the business until he sadly died in 2000. Here, showing off our latest vehicle livery, are Steve Macro, John's successor on the Board, Anthony Saxby, Mike Bell and Bill Saxby, with John in the driving seat. The Board was strengthened around this time by the appointment of our first ever non-executive director, John Millar, who brought much wisdom and experience from his years running Asda's manufacturing division.

Middle The company has continued to support various trade charities over the decades. The Directors have always enjoyed a night out, and in November 1998 they and guests enjoyed an evening of fellowship at the Butchers' and Drovers' Charitable Institute Dinner at the London Hilton in Park Lane. From the left, clockwise, are John Saxby (Director, wearing glasses), Les Peach, Geoff Cobb, Anthony Saxby (Director), Chris Saunders (Executive Management Group member – and great-grandson of Herbert Saxby senior), Bill Saxby (Director), Steve Macro (Director), Jim Saxby (Chairman), Mike Bell (Director), and Malcolm Carter (Drover).

Bottom The company has always acknowledged how much we depend on a well-trained and motivated workforce, and proof of this commitment to our staff came on 22 April 1998 when we first achieved the Investor in People qualification – one of the first companies in our sector to achieve this accreditation. Chairman Jim Saxby was presented with the Award at a ceremony in front on the entire staff. Martyn Wylie, Chief Executive of the Northants Chamber of Commerce, Training and Enterprise, did the honours. As we said at the time, 'The hard work that has been involved demonstrates our confidence in the ability of our staff, at all levels, to continue to develop as the needs and aspirations of the company continue to expand.' Our commitment to the Investor in People philosophy continues just as strongly today.

A century of advertising

Through these pages we have seen a number of adverts for the company's products over the years – particularly pork pies. Here are just a few of our more colourful adverts and promotional material from past and present.

Right This cardboard counter poster dating from the 1940s has become a collectors' item and is available on the internet today for $22.00. The website blurb says: '"Saxby's Delicious Puff Pastry Ready For The Oven" is all that need be said about this product. The picture tells the rest.' I agree.

Below This original 'We recommend SAXBY'S' window sticker first appeared on our Ideal Home Exhibition stand in 1938. It was seen on shop windows up and down the country in the 1950s, '60s and '70s.

Below right There have been various versions of the Saxby Pies sticker since then. This new look came out in the 1990s when the strapline 'FINE FOODS OF DISTINCTION' and new logo came along. Today's logo has changed again – see page 89.

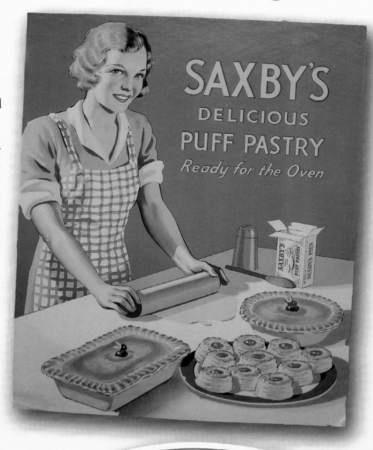

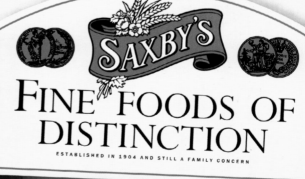

A SPICED APPLE PIE

MUSHROOM & RED PEPPER PIE

Now every TOM, DICK

AND HARRIET CAN

MAKE PERFECT PASTRY.

INDIVIDUAL CHOCOLATE &
ORANGE CHEESECAKES

FRESH AND READY TO USE FROM THE DAIRY CHILLER

Saxby's bring you premium Shortcrust and Puff. They're fresh and ready to use from your Asda dairy chiller (although you can freeze them if you want to). So whatever you make, you can be sure you'll get perfect results every time. With no fuss and no bother. Give Saxby's a try, you're sure to surprise yourself, whatever your name is.

VISIT THE DAIRY CHILLER NOW
20p OFF
only at Asda stores.

Valid until 31/12/96 and only against this product range.

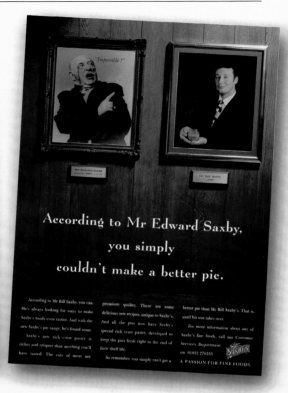

According to Mr Edward Saxby,
you simply
couldn't make a better pie.

According to Mr Bill Saxby, you can. He's always looking for ways to make Saxby's foods even tastier. And with the new Saxby's pie range, he's found some.

Saxby's new rich crust pastry is richer and crisper than anything you'll have tasted. The cuts of meat are premium quality. There are some delicious new recipes, unique to Saxby's. And all the pies now have Saxby's special rich crust pastry, developed to keep the pies fresh right to the end of their shelf life.

So remember, you simply can't get a better pie than Mr Bill Saxby's. That is, until his son takes over.

For more information about any of Saxby's fine foods, call our Customer Services Department on 01933 276333.

A PASSION FOR FINE FOODS.

We hear that fresh pastry is 'in' at the moment.
At Saxby's it's been in for 93 years.

Steak and Kidney Pie

Vegetable and
Cheese Lattice Pie

DELICIOUS SUMMER
FRUIT PIE

Asparagus and Red Onion Tart

Summer Fruit Mille Feuilles

Saxby's commitment to perfection in pastry has lasted four generations. And although we've paid little attention to fashion, we do keep our pastry up to date. You'd expect our range to include the classics of puff and shortcrust pastry. But as a sop to modern life we also offer ready-rolled and lattice to make perfect results even easier. You'll find them all, fresh of course, in the dairy cabinet. And what you don't use, you can simply freeze.

There's history in the making of Saxby's chilled pastry

Opposite far left We have developed some strange promotional ideas over the years. By 1996 we were definitely veering towards the avant-garde when our tongue-in-cheek pastry advertising introduced Tom, Dick and Harriet, all of whom, we are told, make perfect pastry – Saxby's, of course. This particular campaign ran with Asda in the run-up to Christmas that year.

Opposite left 1996 also saw some innovation in the pie department. A 'new' strapline was introduced – 'Saxby's – A Passion For Fine Foods' – and a new range of cold pies was launched. Who better to head this up than Bill Saxby, son of Jim and the first fourth-generation Saxby Director? According to Bill's great-grandfather, Ted, 'You simply couldn't make a better pie.' According to Bill, and the rest of us, we did.

Opposite below By 1997 our pastry marketing was turning to nostalgia. This advert centred on pastry recipes over the last 93 years. 'Saxby's commitment to perfection in pastry has lasted four generations,' says the copy.

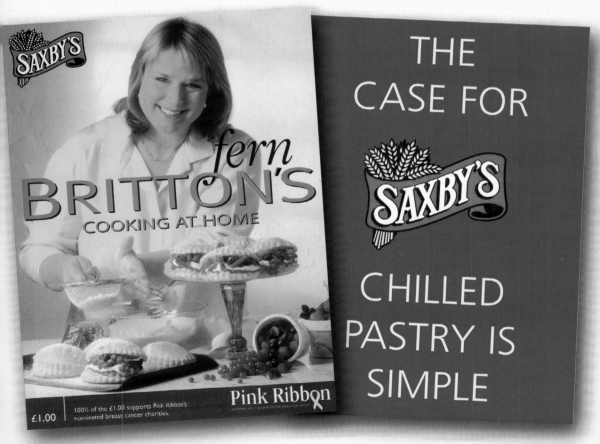

Above One of our most successful link-ups was with Fern Britton in 2000. Publishing this cookbook enabled us to raise funds for the Pink Ribbon charity that year. The cover also features the first appearance of the latest, and current, Saxby's logo.

Above The whole pastry range was brought up to date and re-packaged in 2003, and new lines were introduced. This brochure sleeve promotes our full range of pastry products.

·8·
A new millennium

The start of the new millennium has been a challenge for all food producers as they come to terms with the increasingly competitive market conditions. It has been just as much a challenge for Saxby's. The Board had been joined at the start of 2000 by our new non-executive Director Peter Macielinski, and his appointment was a catalyst for another period of evolution within the business.

We had already decided to focus our attentions on our best customer categories and our best product groups, and this had resulted in quite a change in both customers and products.

In March 2000, this process was well under way. We reflected the changes by forming three divisions: Saxby Filled Products, Saxby Pastry, and Saxby Foodservice. This enabled our teams to give full attention to their own area and also gave our key executives full responsibility, as Divisional Managing Directors, for running their own 'business'.

This brought definite benefits to the company, and at the end of 2001 we moved to a simpler structure with Bill Saxby becoming Managing Director of the whole company. Mike Bell, John Saxby and Peter Macielinski have now retired from the Board, and Brian Homewood was appointed Operations Director in May 2002.

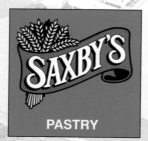

Right Saxby's today continues to be a thriving business. We employ more than 400 people, and turnover is continuing to rise despite the market pressures. We are delighted to still supply most of the major supermarket retailers with our products, and are continuing to develop products for them all the time. We are expanding satisfactorily in our chosen supermarket product groups. Our foodservice business is also developing strongly, and again this involves a number of innovative new product developments. We are also pleased to still have a route to the independent trade through our long-standing distributor, Medallion Chilled Foods of Luton. This aerial photograph was taken in 2000, and shows the entire factory site, with Chester Road in the foreground and Brook Street East in the distance. The original factory is in the top centre of the picture under the white 'northlight' roof. All our extensions over the 80 years since we moved there can be seen. The only significant external development since then has been the creation of the Innovation Centre during 2000, which has given us a first-class facility for product development and customer presentations.

Below Our Swansgate shop closed, on the expiry of its lease, on 30 March 2002, bringing to an end almost a century of Saxby retailing in Wellingborough. It was a great shop and a great facility for the people of Wellingborough, and we were sad when it shut.

Here, manager Dennis Bridge pulls the shutter down to close the shop for the last time. Our very busy factory shop in Brook Street East, managed by Doreen Parker, who is still doing a great job after 43 years of service, is now our last outlet open to the public.

Our factory environment today is a very different world from that of a few years ago. Standards of process and control have never been higher, and although all our lines now have increasing amounts of automation and computerisation, we still rely on our skilled workforce as much as ever, and we put a lot of effort into staff training and development. Today's bakery retains similarities with the old days: this line is making 3lb (1.4kg) pies and can accommodate automatic or hand filling with up to five different layers.

This line is making gala pies, producing more in an hour than the old gala team used to turn out in a day. The factory scheduling is controlled by a computer-aided forecast system, which plans materials throughout the process.

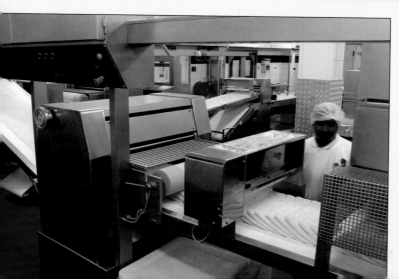

Our pastry production is all highly automated. This is the Rademaker puff pastry laminator, being operated by Chris Atterbury.

Above As we have moved forward over the last couple of years, our management team has also changed quite a bit. We have been pleased to welcome some new faces into the team recently, bringing with them the skills and experience that are needed as we continue to develop our business in the competitive world of today. This is part of the current team: from the left they are Doug Reid, David Hulbert, Derek Powell, Steve Reid, Brian Homewood, Darren Surry, Duncan Amps and Tim Rawlings.

Above right This is our main Board level team today. From the left, Chris Jarvis gives the financial input as Finance Controller, I am Chairman, Bill Saxby fully runs the business on a day-to-day basis as Managing Director, and Brian Homewood is in charge of the entire production process as Operations Director. Some of today's Saxby brand products are laid out before us, including our Centenary Pork Pie and the Centenary Dessert Pastry, two amazing new products for 2004.

Below Finally, the Saxby family, whose input into the business is much less hands-on than it has been in the past. However, our shareholders of today, and they are still nearly all family members, give guidance on long-term strategy but leave implementation to the Board and the professional management team.

The family last gathered en masse in 1994. Almost everyone in this photo, taken on the same lawn at The Lindens as the photo of Herbert Saxby's 1918 welcome home party on page 14, is related either directly or through marriage to the company's founders.

I know that the family share with me a feeling of pride in what has been achieved since that day in 1904 when two brothers took their first step in business together. I also think that those two gentlemen would be pleased with what has happened to their business in the intervening 100 years.

But, being Saxbys, they probably wouldn't say so.

Gold Watch staff, 1920s-2004

The company archives record that six people received gold watches in 1950 in recognition of 30 years' service, and that since then 135 other staff members have received Long Service Awards, taking us up to 2004. Today, the service qualification has been reduced to a mere 20 years!

This is the Saxby Roll of Honour:

Year	Name	Department
1949	Mr Cyril Ashpole	Office
1958	Mr Arthur Sharman	Bakery
1959	Mr Fred Osman	St Albans shop
1959	Mrs Edith Sturgess	Packing
1960	Mr Charlie Jarvis	Abington Square shop
1962	Mr Bill H. Mace	Butchery
1962	Mr Frank Skelton	Van sales
1962	Mrs Elsie Warwick	Canteen
1964	Mr Edgar Watson	Midland Rd shop/Bacon
1964	Mr Arthur Barron	Driver
1964	Mr C. A. (Roger) Cobley	Driver
1964	Mr George Ulyatt	Bakery
1964	Mr Les Clipstone	Packing
1964	Mr Sid Wallis	Bakery
1965	Mr George E. Salter	Bedford shop
1965	Mrs Margaret Salter	Bedford shop
1966	Mr Arthur Weidman	Butchery
1966	Mr Bill Green	Bakery
1967	Mrs Irene E Payne	Bakery
1968	Mrs Sophie Hubble	Bakery
1968	Mrs Marg McLachlen	Packing
1968	Mrs Olive Collins	Butchery
1969	Mrs Dot Dawson	Bakery
1969	Mrs Hilda Bursnall	Office
1969	Mrs Ivy Elson	Bakery
1971	Mr Len Pocock	Bakery
1971	Mr Ron Coles	Bakery
1971	Mrs Pam Hawkes	Bakery
1971	Mrs Betty Desborough	Office
1971	Mrs Chris Bailey	Bakery
1971	Mrs Joyce Grace	Midland Rd shop
1972	Mrs Elsie Fleming	Bakery
1973	Mr Fred C. Brown	Bedford shop
1974	Mr Ken Scott	Cambridge St shop
1974	Mrs Mollie Chambers	Bakery
1975	Miss Dorothy Denton	Bakery
1975	Mrs Edna Bryant	Bakery
1976	Mrs Mary Tysoe	Bakery
1976	Mrs Hilda Kingham	Bakery
1977	Mr Harry Ayes	Butchery
1977	Mrs Pauline Martin	Bakery
1977	Mrs Dorothy Hollis	Packing
1977	Mrs Dora Goodwin	Bakery
1978	Mr Horace Anker	Boilerman
1978	Mrs Alice Halliday	Bakery
1979	Mr Fred Carter	Butchery
1979	Mr Alan Boag	Packing
1979	Mrs Joan Ward	Packing
1980	Mrs Joan Reading	Bakery
1980	Mr Bob Dove	Butchery/Abattoir
1980	Mrs Joan Whitney	Office
1980	Mrs Ena Hayes	Bakery
1980	Mr Fred Bowman	Dunstable shop
1981	Mrs Doreen Parker	Packing
1981	Mrs Ellen Dunkley	Bakery
1981	Mrs Milly Woods	Bakery
1982	Mr John Wright	Bakery
1982	Mrs Margaret Swift	Bakery
1982	Mrs Rhoda Thompson	Bakery
1982	Miss Winnie Lappin	Northampton shop

Year	Name	Department/Shop
1982	Mrs Bunny Warren	St Albans shop
1982	Mrs Gwen (Peggy) Webb	St Albans shop
1983	Mr Harold Ransom	Arndale shop
1983	Mrs Jean Burgess	Arndale shop
1984	Mrs Margaret Moore	Gloucester Place shop
1984	Mrs Joyce Griffin	Gloucester Place shop
1984	Mrs Doreen Ross	Bakery
1984	Mr Brian Dunkley	Abattoir/Engineers
1984	Mr Dennis Salter	Bakery
1984	Mr Eric Orton	Bakery
1985	Mr Bill Brown	Office
1985	Mr Harry Sebastian	Bakery
1985	Mr Keith Haddon	Bakery
1985	Mr Terry Jackson	St Albans shop
1985	Mrs Rosemary Green	Dunstable shop
1985	Mrs June Hicklin	Packing
1986	Mr Brian Wells	Bedford shop
1986	Mr Andy Harris	Butchery
1986	Mrs Edna Clarke	Rushden shop
1986	Mrs Marion Parsons	Bedford shop
1986	Mrs Jean Fowler	St Albans shop
1986	Miss Jean Smeathers	Bakery
1986	Mrs Marg Schreter	Bakery
1986	Mrs Nancy Fordham	Office
1987	Mr David Horn	Butchery
1987	Mr David Paling	Bakery
1987	Mr David Rice	Bakery
1987	Mrs Doreen Ziabeck	Sausage
1987	Mrs Barbara West	Packing
1988	Mr Keith Freeland	Arndale/Bacon dept
1988	Mrs Sandra Stephenson	Rushden shop/Pastry
1989	Mr Ian Wilson	Driver
1989	Mrs Janet Pell	Thrapston shop
1989	Mrs Mary Salter	Packing
1990	Mrs Pam Mitchell	Packing
1990	Mr Stan May	Office
1990	Mr Eric Coles	Packing
1990	Mrs June Rowland	Bakery
1990	Mrs Lena Clemanzi	Bakery
1990	Mr Phil Stapleton	Stores
1990	Mrs Zophie Benderz	Packing
1991	Mr Bryan Martin	Office
1992	Mrs Marilyn Dunkley	Office
1992	Mrs Janice King	Bakery
1993	Mr Gerald Lawrence	Bakery
1993	Mr Stuart Johnson	Butchery/Hygiene
1994	Mr Dudley Waples	Bakery
1994	Mrs Kathy Page	Bakery
1994	Mrs Pat Horn	Sausage
1995	Mrs Anne Williams	Bakery
1996	Mrs Barbara Drage	Packing/Laundry
1996	Miss Irene Branston	Bakery
1996	Mrs M. Chrissy Auriemma	Bakery
1997	Mr Marcus Sebastian	Bakery
1997	Mr Paul Tweed	Butchery
1997	Mr Jim Askew	Abattoir/Meat prep
1997	Mrs Angie Minter	Bakery/Planning
1997	Miss Mary Rudd	Bakery
1998	Mr Graham Driscoll	Driver
1998	Mr Howard Smith	Bakery
1998	Mr Ian Haddon	Packing
1998	Mr Janti Patel	Butchery
1998	Mr Colin Park-Neal	Pastry
1998	Mrs I. Margaret Iaconianni	Bakery
1998	Miss Margaret Berrill	Bakery/Pastry
1999	Mr Andrew Dove	Butchery
1999	Mr Sean Weed	Butchery
1999	Mr Keith Parr	Bakery
1999	Mrs José Jones	Bakery
2000	Mr Mark Salter	Driver/Packing
2000	Mr Chitran Patel	Bakery
2000	Mr John Coode	Driver
2000	Mr Mick Campbell	Electrician
2002	Mr Sid Eady	Engineers
2003	Mr Chris Saunders	Sales/Training

Saxby family tree

The full Saxby family tree dating back to our founders' generation would today include hundreds of names. Our tree focuses on just the two founders and those of their family members who have been Directors of the business and who are the current shareholders. I apologise that space limitations mean I have not been able to include everyone, especially the many fifth-generation children.

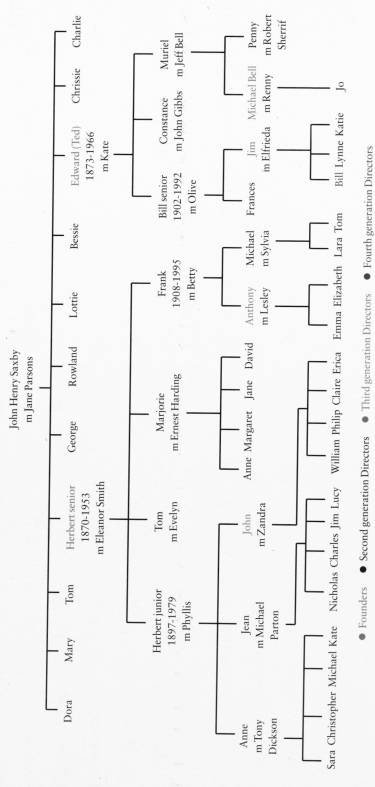

John Henry Saxby
m Jane Parsons

Dora   Mary   Tom   Herbert senior   George   Rowland   Lottie   Bessie   Edward (Ted)   Chrissie   Charlie
                        1870-1953   1873-1966
                        m Eleanor Smith   m Kate

Herbert junior   Tom   Marjorie   Frank   Bill senior   Constance   Muriel
1897-1979   m Evelyn   m Ernest Harding   1908-1995   1902-1992   m John Gibbs m Jeff Bell
m Phyllis   m Betty   m Olive

Jean   John   Anne Margaret Jane David   Anthony   Michael   Frances   Jim   Michael Bell   Penny
m Michael m Zandra   m Lesley m Sylvia   m Elfrieda m Renny   m Robert
Parton   Sherrif

Anne   Jo
m Tony
Dickson

Sara Christopher Michael Kate   Nicholas Charles Jim Lucy   William Philip Claire Erica   Emma Elizabeth   Lara Tom   Bill Lynne Katie

● Founders   ● Second generation Directors   ● Third generation Directors   ● Fourth generation Directors

96